# Get to know SCOTLAND'S FORESTS

# Get to know SCOTLAND'S FORESTS

**Peter Ross**

**Macdonald Publishers, Edinburgh**

**The Melven Press, Perth**

©Peter Ross 1982

Designed and edited by Jenny Carter

Published by
Macdonald Publishers
Loanhead, Midlothian
EH20 9SY
and
The Melven Press
176 High Street
Perth
PH1 1QA

ISBN 0904 265 501 (cased)
        0904 265 51 X (paperback)

Printed in Scotland by
Macdonald Printers (Edinburgh) Limited,
Edgefield Road, Loanhead, Midlothian
EH20 9SY

# Contents

# Acknowledgements

I am indebted to the following for their help and assistance:

The Forestry Commission, in particular the Information Branch, for general guidance and a supply of literature; their photographic library for the photographs used on pages 18, 20, 23, 24, 25, 26, 30, 34, 45, 49, 65, 84, 90, 105 and 116; the Recreation Officer, South Scotland Conservancy, for assistance, and for the use of photographs of Galloway; Mr Desmond Dugan of Taynuilt for the pictures on pages 123 and 136, and Mr Milligan for the picture on page 73. Jennifer MacLeod, who helped me with typing; Jenny Carter, the editor, and the publishers for their help and encouragement and finally, my wife, family, colleagues and friends who listened, encouraged and gave me useful advice.

# Preface

The Forestry Commission is the biggest single landowner in the country and has since 1968 been steadily increasing the recreational facilities available in its forests. In today's stringent financial climate the scope for new developments is limited and priority is being given to providing facilities in woodlands close to towns. For many years the Forestry Commission has allowed access to its forests for pedestrians; even before the war it created Forest Parks where recreation and access were to be given an important place. Today the Commission has in Scotland 9 campsites, 122 picnic places, 231 forest walks, 11 visitor centres, 5 arboreta, 2 forest drives, and 87 forest cabins and holiday houses.

On top of that the private landowner has responded by opening up many mansion houses and castles with their beautiful policy woods. The National Trust for Scotland has many fine buildings and policies in its care. The Nature Conservancy has many reserves in which there are visitor centres and nature trails.

I spent my teenage weekends climbing, camping, and walking all over Scotland. After I married and had a family this was no longer possible except for brief holidays; instead, we started to explore all the forest walks and policy woods round about where we lived at that particular time. I still find peace and relaxation in the woods in spite of my work as a forester. I want to share my enjoyment with you, as there is plenty of room in the forest for everyone to find a quiet corner with a distant view. Hence this book, designed to guide you round the very large selection of walks available. I hope it contributes to your enjoyment of our national resource.

# I

# Forestry
# in
# Scotland

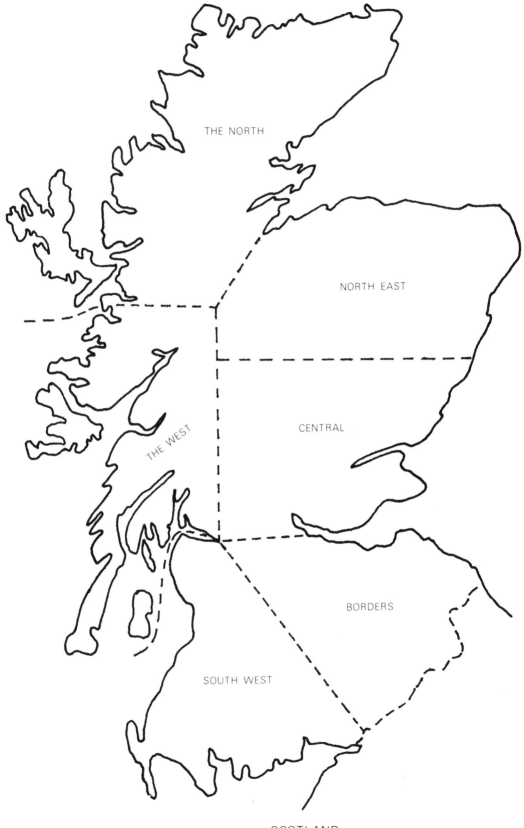

THE NORTH

NORTH EAST

THE WEST

CENTRAL

BORDERS

SOUTH WEST

SCOTLAND

# A Forest

Technically, a forest is a wood or collection of woods and plantations managed to provide a continuous supply of timber. The popular concept is either of some large primeval wood straight out of a fairy tale, or of a large coniferous plantation of modern origin. Whether the forest is "natural" or a man-made plantation, modern forest management aims at a perpetuation of a forest environment. This book looks at a man-made forest and how it is worked and managed, and at Scotland's sad remnants of its once large primeval forests, and describes the major species found there today.

With the increase in car ownership and a shorter working week Scotland's expanding forests were under increasing pressure from a growing number of visitors. This was formally recognised in the Countryside (Scotland) Act of 1967 when the Commission was charged "to provide certain recreational or sporting facilities on land placed at their disposal." From that date there has been a steady build up of a large range of facilities. A forest can offer a large number of visitors comparative privacy, and it should be remembered that most forests are in areas of outstanding scenic beauty. They are not suited for activities which require a large number of spectators; individuals or small groups must be allowed to enjoy quiet rural activities such as walking, fishing, or merely observing nature. This has become an important aspect of forest management, and an aim that has been endorsed by successive governments.

The main rôle of a forest, however, has to be the production of timber and the resulting stimulation of the local rural economy. This is the forester's priority, and all other management considerations are fitted round it. What can happen is that in certain places where visitor pressure is high, recreation becomes an important management consideration so that, for example, a fine stand of trees near a popular picnic place will be retained for as long as possible.

Today's forest is an area of land set aside to grow trees for timber, so that the land supports a local staff of workers who help to keep the villages alive and the schools open. It also provides a recreational area where people can walk, camp, picnic, observe nature, shoot, and enjoy a pleasant view.

# The Place of Forestry

Scotland was once a well-forested country from the Borders northwards. We know this from pollen analysis and, more visibly, from stumps turned out by peat cutting all over the country. No one can say precisely how much of Scotland was covered by forest as it altered from climatic period to climatic period; it has been suggested that perhaps fifty per cent of the country was covered in trees — approximately five times as much as today. The Romans knew of "Silva Caledonia" because it proved too difficult a province for them to settle permanently. A possible origin of the word

"Caledonia" is from the Gaelic *coille dun* meaning "wooded strongholds" or "forts of the woods." Today when the word is used it refers only to the remnants of native pine forest.

The species found in that forest would vary according to climate and location but would include all our native broadleaves such as oak and birch which flourished in the better soils and weather of ground below 150 metres in the south and west. In the north and east and on higher ground elsewhere our native conifers — pine, juniper, and yew would be more common.

The disappearance of this forest can be attributed to good farming practices. As society became more complex and numerous a shift from a hunting-based occupation to a more settled agrarian one took place and with it the need for more food from more efficient farming. At first this occurred round the existing communities, with more forest being cleared for tillage. This ground would be enclosed from the grazing animals who would forage in the surrounding woods, thereby denuding that area of young trees. When the old trees died, therefore, there were no saplings to take their place. As the grazing of animals became more important, and therefore organised, in upland areas so the practice of muirburn became more frequent. "Muirburn" is the burning off of old vegetation in the spring so that a fresh green bite may be provided that little bit earlier. The introductions by the medieval monastic orders of organised sheep husbandry did much to deplete our forest area. The biggest concentration of monasteries were found in the Borders, which is today associated with sheep and textiles, and where there are virtually no native woods.

The commercial exploitation of Scotland's forests did not really begin to take place until the eighteenth century when an export trade to England was set up because of the scarcity of wood there. Commercial ventures such as iron-smelting, which needed vast quantities of charcoal, were tried in the Highlands, as at Furnace on Loch Fyne. Perhaps mention should be made of more dramatic acts of depredation occasionally chronicled, such as the burning of huge tracts of forest to get rid of wolves or outlaws. These fires no doubt occurred, witness the fire blackened pines in Glenmore, but the accuracy of these accounts should be treated sceptically as definitive areas are never given, and history tends to be a record of the dramatic.

Organised forestry in Scotland is quite well documented. In the sixteenth century a number of Royal Acts stated that every laird was obliged in law to establish an acre of wood wherever there was none. These Acts, however, had little effect, and it was left to the individual landowners such as Sir Duncan Campbell from Breadalbane, the fourth Duke of Atholl, and Archibald Grant of Monymusk to start extensive plantations. Scotsmen were in the forefront of scientific forestry. Allied institutions and societies were founded before comparable English ones; the Royal Botanic Garden in Edinburgh was founded in 1680, eighty years before that at Kew. Archibald Menzies was botanist with Captain Vancouver's Pacific Expedition and discovered among other species Sitka Spruce in 1792. Subsequently David Douglas was sent to explore North West America for suitable species to introduce to this country. These were Sitka Spruce, Douglas Fir, and Lodgepole Pine. An Edinburgh group of landowners, known as the Oregon Association, sent John Jeffrey to America from where he introduced Western Hemlock. Another Scottish collector, William Murray, sent Lawson's cypress to an Edinburgh nurseryman. The Royal Scottish Forestry Society was founded in 1854, twenty-seven years before its English counterpart. Finally Edinburgh University was the first in the country to appoint a lecturer in forestry in 1889. All these people and events were the foundations upon which modern plantation forestry as practised in this century has been built.

Despite this, there had never been in this country an effective central forestry policy such as some European countries have had for centuries; and World War I found our dwindling supplies of wood severely depleted. In 1919 the Forestry Commission was set up as a government agency to plant and encourage planting to provide a strategic reserve of timber. The main impetus occurred after World War II when once again this country did not have enough wood.

In 1981 Scotland had 921,000 hectares of woodlands which represents twelve per cent of the total land surface. This figure comprises of 798,000 hectares of coniferous plantations, 39,000 of managed broadleaved plantations, and 84,000 of unproductive woodland. (Note: 1 hectare equals approximately 2½ acres). The most afforested region of Scotland is Dumfries and Galloway with sixteen per cent of the total area under trees. If we compare this to other countries we find that Denmark has twelve per cent, Italy twenty-seven per cent, France twenty-five per cent, West Germany thirty per cent, Norway twenty-nine per cent, Japan sixty-seven per cent and Finland seventy-four per cent. Our low area of· forests, the difficulty of exploiting what remains of the world's natural forests, the raising of the price in a seller's market, the fact that we can only supply eight per cent of wood used in this country should surely provide a strong argument for a soundly-based home supply of what is a renewable resource.

# Forestry Practice

Forestry is, like farming, all about how to get as much as possible out of the ground in successive crops. The difference comes about because instead of taking a year from seed to harvest, the forester expects a crop rotation of forty to sixty years for conifers and one hundred to two hundred years for broadleaves. This means that unlike the farmer the forester cannot improve his soil by cultivation every year but can only improve his soil once in the life of his crop. The long crop rotation also means that it is very difficult to refute criticism, as the proof of the forester's argument does not materialise for fifty years. I am definitely on the side of the trees. To my mind the need for trees and timber will always be with us no matter how advanced our technology becomes; and wood is one of our few renewable resources unlike coal and oil which are a finite resource. To plant a tree is a definite act of optimism for the future of mankind, for it will be used long after the planter's death. Whether it will be still sawn into planks for housebuilding or processed into some other product is something about which to speculate when you are walking through the forest.

What I hope to do here is explain a little about the practice of forestry so that you will have a greater understanding of what the forester is doing. He starts with a bare hillside, which in this country is normally bought on the free market. This ground has to be surveyed for information about the soil, slopes, drainage patterns, exposure and elevation, and to ascertain the legal boundaries. With this information the forester can then make decisions about choice of species, type of cultivation, drainage systems, planting limits, position and type of fence. He also has to take into account when making these decisions the restraints of finance, public amenity, local land-use considerations, and landscaping. Having made these decisions he then has to go about organising the operations so that a plantation will be created.

# The Operations

## Choice of Species

This is done by using soil types so that the correct species of tree can be selected for optimum growth. This can be simply done by using plant indicators. For example, cotton grass will only grow on deep undrained peat bogs, while soft meadow grass will indicate a moist fertile soil usually associated with valley bottoms. In most places in Scotland, the forester's choice will fall on Sitka Spruce as it is the fastest-growing of our conifers over the greatest range of sites. The landscaping and amenity considerations, if applicable, will cause him to select some larch to highlight some important aspect of the landform, and to plant some broadleaves on suitable ground near a public road. Thereafter he will arrange the delivery of the correct number of the preferred species from the nursery.

## Fencing and Cultivation

The fence will have to be sited and constructed to give small trees the maximum protection from danger. In the Highlands this will be shared by sheep and red deer, while in the south the main damaging agents are sheep and cattle. To protect against deer a fence must be at least six feet high and should be sited so that snow will not build up and bury it. A stock fence, on the other hand, need only be three or four feet high. In both cases, it is essential to allow downfalls from the high tops during winter for the animals.

To cultivate the ground a forester will use one of the specialised forestry ploughs which have been developed during the past thirty years. These ploughs will provide the young plant with a favoured planting spot which has local drainage and some weed suppression. To do this safely the machine must travel straight up and down the hill across the contour. These dark ribbons are always criticised for looking unsightly but they will only last a couple of years at the most. In the past it was considered efficient if breaks (called rides) were straight and management units (called compartments) were small and regular; but with the advent of increased

*An MF 400 tractor ploughing land in North Scotland prior to planting Lodgepole Pine.*

mechanisation and increasing awareness of landscaping considerations, this is no longer the case. Rides now follow natural boundaries like burns and follow the contour so that they are not so intrusive, while compartments are now much larger.

It is during this operation that the forester considers the question of planting limits. In the west where the exposure is normally severe planting will not go much above 1000 feet (300 metres). In the south and east, planting frequently goes as high as 1,700 feet (500 metres). Here landscaping plays an important part in the decision, because the top planting line is very crucial, as is the legal boundary. At the simplest these are straight lines, but the forester will plan the ploughing so that the resulting plantation will be more in sympathy with the underlying landform. The trees will not be planted at the 1000 (300 metre) contour, but will follow the spurs and saddles. If the fence line is straight down a prominent hillside then the plantation will not follow it but come inside it and the resultant bare ground will, if possible, be planted with broadleaves. This is now being done, but just as the present-day forester is being criticised for the 1950s plantings, so his own forest landscaping will not be seen for another twenty years or so.

Public amenity also has to be identified at this time, and the appropriate action taken, so that well-used footpaths are not ploughed and planted. Likely walks and picnic places are assessed and the correct treatment applied. Important viewpoints are remembered and retained.

# Planting

To plant the trees the forester has to get plants and workers together at the planting site, in the right weather, at the right time of the year. The right time of year in upland Scotland is from the end of February until the middle of May, so the danger of hard frosts or dry spells has to be watched. One worker during this period can be expected to plant about twenty-five to thirty hectares if all the planting is on ploughing. He or she will do this by carrying a bundle of one hundred plants in a special bag, cutting a notch in the plough ridge with a spade, inserting the plant, and firming with the foot.

The newly-created plantation will then have to be fertilised by helicopter, weeded for a couple of years, dead trees replaced, and the plantation protected from fire and browsing animals.

The plantation then goes into a waiting period, during which time it will be top-dressed with fertiliser by helicopter. The length of the wait depends on a management decision about whether the plantation will

*Felling mature timber.* be thinned or left to be felled. The factors influencing this decision are the rate and growth of the trees, the soil, the exposure, amenity factors and the degree of difficulty of harvesting. This aspect has become very sophisticated through years of study; today's forester can manage the harvesting and marketing of his forest by his knowledge of the standing volumes, their size ranges and whether these match the model so that the stand will be felled at the right time to maximise the financial return.

# Felling

The felling of conifers will take place when they are between forty and sixty years old. It will probably be carried out by a man using a chainsaw who will cut around twenty to forty trees a day, depending on the size of the tree. He will sned (remove branches) the tree using the same saw and, depending on the extraction system employed, will cross-cut the tree into logs either in the wood or at roadside.

There are two types of extraction (moving the wood from stump to road). In the mountainous areas of the west and north where the slopes are steep cableway machines are used, capable of extracting about 100 tonnes of logs a week. Where the ground is not so steep, special tractors are used which can extract about 250 to 400 tonnes a week.

These two jobs are probably the forester's most difficult tasks, so much is being done to mechanise the operation. This is quite a task, as the system requires highly skilled operators, a very large annual programme of around 70,000 tonnes, and finally about £300,000 to buy the machines.

There are four machines. A *feller-buncher*, which fells and stacks the trees for the *grapple bunk skidder* to move to the *processor*, which debranches and cross-cuts the tree into logs. A *forwarder* will then move the wood to where the specialised timber lorry can take the wood to the mill. The whole operation can then begin all over again, except that the planting will be called a restocking.

# Forest Recreation

The recreational facilities available in our forests are varied but all are country based so are quiet and informal in nature. The Forestry Commission in particular recognised the potential early on and has always allowed pedestrians free access to the forests. The Commission also created Forest Parks – Argyll in 1935, Galloway in 1943, Glen More in 1948, and Queen Elizabeth in 1953. These have formed the basis for the expansion of recreational facilities in the seventies.

## Campsites

There are nine major campsites provided by the Forestry Commission throughout the country. In addition to these the Commission leases a number of sites to the Camping Club of Great Britain and, of course, there are plenty of sites available with splendid forest settings so a check in an up-to-date map will show what forests are nearby.

The Commission's nine sites are graded according to the facilities they offer. There are six class A sites which have flush toilets and showers, while the three class B sites have limited facilities and campers must provide their own toilet facilities. There is, too, one back-packers' site – an area on which camping is permitted. (I must say here that I am a very reluctant user of organised campsites. Family responsibilities are forcing me to find flush toilets and washing facilities when we now go camping although I would like to see a series of linked back-packing campsites through our larger forests.) The Commission also has sites available for schools and other youth organisations.

| | | | |
|---|---|---|---|
| **Caldons** | Glen Trool Forest | Galloway | Class A |
| **Kilvrecht** | Rannoch Forest | Upper Tayside | Class B |
| **Cobleland** | Loch Ard Forest | Stirlingshire | Class A |
| **Cashel** | Buchanan Forest | Loch Lomondside | Class A |
| **Talnotry** | Kirroughtry Forest | Galloway | Class B |
| **Ardgartan** | Ardgartan Forest | Argyll Forest Park | Class A |
| **Glencoe** | Glencoe Forest | Glencoe | Class A |
| **Glenmore** | Glenmore Forest | Cairngorms | Class A |
| **Balmacara** | South Strome Forest | Kintail | Class B |

Both classes take caravans and tents and can be busy during the season. Charges vary from year to year so if this concerns you write to the Commission or call at your nearest Forest for the current year's price leaflet. Charges in 1980 varied from £1 to £2.50 per camper per night.

*Talnotry Campsite is set in the heart of the Galloway hills.*

My own favourite site is Talnotry in Galloway. The situation is its most appealing feature with its steep rocky hill on one side, the forested hill on the other, and a splendid burn running along the bottom of the site.

# Holiday Houses

The Forestry Commission's holiday houses fall into two groups; first, houses which are not required for workers and are fully fitted and furnished for the holiday trade, and second, custom built log cabins which are built on one site with a comprehensive collection of facilities such as shop, television room, laundry and information displays. If you are thinking of using the cabins contact the Forestry Commission early in the year to get the booking forms. These have to be sent to Edinburgh no matter where you are thinking of going and the earlier you book the better as the cabins are popular.

*Strathyre Forest Cabins on the shores of Loch Lubnaig.*

The houses are mainly in two centres, the forestry villages of *Glentrool* and *Dalavich* and are semi-

detached. The facilities offered at the cabins are not available here. There are a few single houses available.

In all the houses and cabins the availability of long weekend bookings is there throughout the year. For youth groups there is, at Glenmore, a hostel for hire known as the Norwegian Hostel which has 46 beds.

*A Forest Cabin on Lochaweside, secluded and pretty.*

*Breakfast on the verandah — Lochaweside.*

## Cost Range
## (1981/2)

| Name | Type | High Season | Low Season | Number of units | Number of beds |
|---|---|---|---|---|---|
| **Lochaweside** | Cabin | £175 | £65 | 44 | 5/6 |
| **Strathyre** | Cabin | £170 | £55 | 17 | 5 |
| **Glentrool** | House | £115 | £40 | 14 | 5 |
| **Dalavich** | House | £135 | £45 | 17 | 5 |
| **Achnamara** | House | £120 | £40 | 1 | 5 |
| **Tigh Na Coille** | House | £155 | £65 | 1 | 6 |
| **Kinshaldy** | House | £155 | £65 | 1 | 6 |

# Walks

There are around 200 walks and trails in Scotland's forests. These vary from the short stroll on a gravel path round a loch to a twelve-mile traverse of the mountains. Over the course of many years I have walked many miles on various routes, and in addition to listing all the walks available, I have given fuller details of some that have impressed me (or not as the case may be) or that I would recommend.

A word of advice about the walks and how to interpret the usually excellent guides that are available: look first at the distance to judge whether you can manage to complete the whole walk in the time you have available. A rough guide is to allow about a half hour for every mile. If you are very fit twenty minutes is adequate, or if you are taking a young family you should allow forty minutes. On a trail, however, you should allow up to an hour a mile to give yourself time to read and follow the descriptions. Generally speaking a "walk" will be relatively short and a guide not essential if you are to get full enjoyment from the walk.

Grading a walk is the most difficult thing in the world as no two graders would agree on the same walk. This is where the attention to detail given by management comes across most strongly, but there is nothing like thinking for yourself in these circumstances and by using my guide list you should be able to grade your chosen walk yourself before you begin.

**1   Geographical Location**   Argyll where it will be wet and rough or Berwickshire where it will be dryer and smoother.

**2   Description**   A walk to viewpoint usually means a climb while a walk round a loch will be flat.

**3   Ground Conditions**   Check the narrative in your guide carefully for mention of this. An exhortation to wear "stout footwear" usually means that the path will be wet and/or rough. Generally, though, all forests are rough places to walk. The degree will vary with the location and the time of year.

This question concerning "stout footwear" perplexes the inexperienced country walker. My opinion is that to

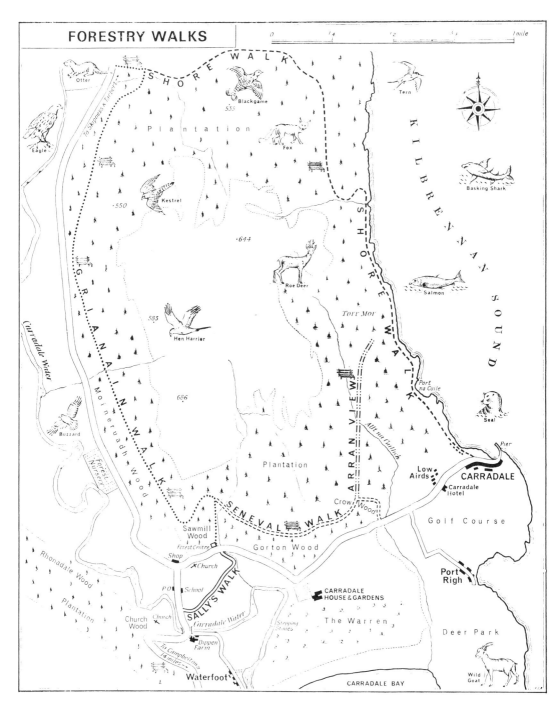

*A sample of a map of a Forest Walk*

enjoy Forest walks you do not need to go to great expense to kit you and your family out with proper walking boots. I would recommend a pair of wellington boots for all of you. I wear them all the time for about ninety per cent of my walking these days. I would not contemplate climbing any of our mountains in wellingtons but I, and countless other country workers, will wear them to wander about the lower slopes of these self same mountains. If you get smitten by the walking bug then by all means buy a good pair of boots because then you will want to tackle more ambitious walks and climbs. Remember it can rain, so have a waterproof in your bag.

You must always remember the *Country Code*:

---

Guard against all risk of fires
Fasten all gates
Keep dogs under proper control
Avoid damaging fences, hedges and walls
Leave no litter
Safeguard water supplies
Protect wildlife, wild plants and trees
Go carefully on country roads
Respect the life of the countryside

---

Fire can devastate a forest and in the spring when the danger is greatest, a considerable part of the forester's work is protecting the plantations from fire. So if you come across a walk closed during that time of year please obey the sign. Most fires are caused by forest visitors and the average annual loss in Scotland is around 300 hectares (about 600,000 trees). If you smoke, make sure that you break your match before you throw it away and stub your cigarette on your heel or on a stone and rub the whole butt between your fingers before throwing it away. That way you can be sure you will not accidentally start a fire. You should never light a fire in a forest at any time of the year.

# Information

One of the Forestry Commission's objectives is to advance knowledge and understanding of forestry and trees in the countryside. By linking this with the aim to provide recreational facilities, the Commission has set up twelve information centres and six arboreta throughout Scotland. Where it is thought that an educational need can be fulfilled whether from a large recreational complex, visitor pressure, or a residential school, Forest Trails have been laid out. Here the participant can be informed of relevant natural aspects along a waymarked walk. The Commission also publish a range of booklets on all aspects of Forestry. Some of these are available at the bigger information centres, main offices, and campsites. If you are really keen you should write to Headquarters in Edinburgh (address list at the back of the book) which can supply you with a complete list. The Nature Conservancy Council also regards it a duty to educate the public and at most of

*The David Marshall Lodge near Aberfoyle: a couple enjoy a stroll around the waterfall trail.*

their reserves, in addition to a booklet being available, wardens are available to conduct parties round the reserve. There are also commercial enterprises such as the Landmark Centre at Carrbridge where their displays and trails have an educational content.

Forestry as an industry is best explained at Forestry information centres. These range from the very large and busy such as The David Marshall Lodge near Aberfoyle to the locally-run centre such as the one at Fleet Forest, in Galloway. For knowledge of individual tree species a visit should be made to either of the Commission's own arboreta where the primary emphasis is on research but where visitors are welcome. The Royal Botanic Gardens in Edinburgh and its two annexes at Benmore, near Dunoon and Logan, near Stranraer are definitely worth visiting to see fine specimens of our more exotic trees. Armed with this knowledge a visit to the policies and woods of our big houses will be much more rewarding.

# Picnic Sites

Scotland's forests are usually in areas of great scenic beauty which are now within easy reach of the car owning public. Studies have shown that the average forest visitor only moves about five metres from his car. To meet this need well over a hundred picnic sites have been laid out by the Forestry Commission with many more being established by local authorities, the National Trust and other bodies. Some, in very crowded areas like Loch Lomondside are just large car parks. Others, such as Loch Linnhe Picnic Place, provide an off the road stopping place of real beauty. Yet others are secreted away in the forest and give one or two families a beautifully private place to have a meal; a good example is Kirriereoch in Galloway. Local authorities such as Dumbarton District Council have used a new road alignment on Loch Lomondside to provide a much needed stopping place. Even this very large picnic site is overcrowded during the local holidays and plans exist to construct further such sites as a new road is constructed up the loch side.

# List of Forestry Commission Fishing

| Name | Type | Forest | Boats |
|------|------|--------|-------|
| Loch Coille Bharr | Trout | Knapdale | Yes |
| Loch Barnluasgan | Trout | Knapdale | Yes |
| Loch Linnhe | Trout | Knapdale | Yes |
| Loch Losgunn | Trout | Knapdale | No |
| Loch Seafield | Trout | Knapdale | No |
| Carse Burn | Sea Trout | Achaglachgach | No |
| Loch Awe | Salmon, Trout | Inverliever | Yes |
| Loch Avich | Trout | Inverliever | Yes |
| River Avich | Trout, Salmon | Inverliever | No |
| Loch Nant | Trout | Inverliever | No |
| Loch Tromlee | Trout | Inverliever | No |
| Cam Loch | Trout | Interliever | No |
| River Liever | Trout, Salmon | Inverliever | No |
| Hospital Lochan | Trout | Glencoe | No |
| Glen Dubh Reservior | Trout | Barcaldine | Yes |
| Loch Dubh Mor | Trout | Barcaldine | No |
| River Goil | Trout, Salmon | Ardgartan | No |
| River Finnart | Trout, Salmon | Benmore | No |
| Loch Drunkie | Trout, Pike | Achray | No |
| Loch Achray | Trout, Pike | Achray | No |
| Loch Reoidhte | Trout | Achray | No |
| Loch Chon | Trout | Loch Ard | Yes |

Information for the above from:
Forestry Commission, Portcullis House, India Street,
Glasgow G2 4PL.

| Name | Type | Forest | Boats |
|------|------|--------|-------|
| Loch Dee | Trout | Galloway | No |
| Black Loch | Trout | Galloway | No |
| Loch of the Lowes | Trout | Galloway | No |
| Lilie's Loch | Trout | Galloway | No |
| Polmaddie Burn | Trout | Galloway | No |
| Water of Minnoch | Trout/Salmon | Galloway | No |
| Loch Bradon | Trout | Carrick | Yes |
| Loch Skelloch | Trout | Carrick | Yes |
| River Stinchar | Trout/Salmon | Carrick | No |
| Breckbowie Loch | Trout | Carrick | Yes |
| Dhu Loch | Pike | Carrick | No |
| Spectacle Loch | Coarse | Penninghame | No |
| Garwackie Loch | Coarse | Penninghame | No |

Information concerning the above lochs from:
Forestry Commission, 55/57 Moffat Road,
Dumfries DG1 1NP.

| Name | Type | Forest | Boats |
|------|------|--------|-------|
| Aigas Loch | Trout | Affric | Yes |
| Loch Morlich | Trout | Glenmore | Yes |

Information for the above from:
Forestry Commission, 21 Church Street,
Inverness IV1 1EL

# Fishing

Fishing is this country's biggest participatory sport. I am not a devotee, though I have dangled a worm on occasion, and my name is synonymous with a Loch Tay salmon fly. The Forestry Commission has done its bit to provide facilities for the angler by having over forty different locations where one can obtain a day permit to fish. Some are rivers, but most are lochs usually with boats available for hire, and all are for fly fishing only. In addition, where the Commission has leased fishing to local associations a condition of that lease is that a number of day tickets must be made available to the general public. Overleaf is a list of Forestry Commission fishing locations. For any other within the forest area the local tourist office will be able to help you.

*Landing a trout on Loch Awe.*

# Horse Riding

There are many opportunities to go riding in the forest but because there is a certain amount of organisation required the individual member of the public might find it a bit difficult. His best bet is to find out if there are any stables or pony-trekking centres near the forest of his choice and arrange his horse riding through them. Most likely they will have some arrangement with the forest. For the local owner his neighbouring forest will arrange a permit for him to use the waymarked bridle-path.

# Shooting

This is a specialised pastime and the individual can only be catered for by the issue of day permits for deer stalking to experienced stalkers. Contact Forestry Commission Headquarters (address at the back) for details. Rough Shootings are occasionally let out for a period of years and once again you should contact Headquarters.

# Wildlife Observation

There are two wildlife enclosures in Galloway, where it is hoped that the general public can catch a glimpse of either deer or goats. To help the more enthusiastic two observation hides have been built and may be used for a fee. These hides may be used for photography for which a fee will be charged. If you are really keen you can arrange for a Forestry Commission Ranger to take you out for a specific stalk.

# Orienteering

The Forestry Commission has set out four orienteering type courses suitable for all ages and called them *Wayfaring Courses*. Basically they are for orienteering without the time element. I am quite excited by the concept as it allows the individual to walk round the forest the way he wants by selecting his own route between points with the use of a master map. He can go as fast or as slow as he wishes, or even leave out most of the points. Clubs and groups can arrange to hold competitions over these courses. The facility is available at the following forests: *Achray*, West Conservancy;

*Glentress*, South Conservancy; *Kirkhill*, East Conservancy; *Glenmore*, North Conservancy.

# Motoring

There are two Forest Drives open to all, one in Galloway, the other in the Trossachs; here, for a small charge, you can drive along a forest road in your own car and picnic along the route.

It is recognised that car rallying does interfere with the quiet enjoyment that can be had in the forest, but without the use of our forest roads this country would not be able to stage any major international rallies. The Commission therefore allows only those rallies which are organised through the Royal Automobile Club, and for which an agreed charge is applied.

# Insects

I find the aerosol repellents effective protection, provided you treat yourself before you go out. Midges are a nuisance, no more, and unless you are especially allergic to their bite a little planning can reduce the degree of irritability by not exposing yourself in sheltered parts at dusk unnecessarily and by using repellent. For those of you camping or caravanning, I find those little bits of Japanese wood called Moon Tiger Mosquito Coils very effective. The only drawback is that you smell constantly of woodsmoke.

# Addresses

I have tried throughout the book to use local addresses and telephone numbers but you may find the following addresses useful.

*Forestry Commission Headquarters,*
231 Corstorphine Road, Edinburgh EH12 7AT, *Tel* 031-334 0303.

*Forestry Commission North Conservancy*,
21 Church Street, Inverness IV1 1EL, *Tel* 0463 32811.

*Forestry Commission East Conservancy*,
6 Queen's Gate, Aberdeen AB9 2NQ, *Tel* 0224 33361.

*Forestry Commission South Conservancy*,
55/57 Moffat Road, Dumfries DG1 1NE,
*Tel* 0387 2425.

*Forestry Commission West Conservancy*,
Portcullis House, 21 India Street, Glasgow G2 4PL,
*Tel* 041 248 3931.

*National Trust for Scotland*, 5 Charlotte Square,
Edinburgh EH2 4DN, *Tel* 031 447 4784.

*Nature Conservancy Council*, 12 Hope Terrace,
Edinburgh EH9 2AS, *Tel* 031 226 5922.

*Countryside Commission for Scotland,*
Battleby House, Redgorton, Perth PH1 3EW,
*Tel* 0738 27921.

*Scottish Tourist Board*, 23 Ravelston Terrace,
Edinburgh EH4 3EU, *Tel* 031 332 2433.

*Royal Society for the Protection of Birds*,
17 Regent Terrace, Edinburgh EH7 5BN,
*Tel* 031 556 5624.

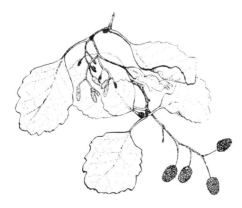

# II

# A
# Guide to
# the
# Forests

FIRTH OF FORTH

Dunbar

HOPETOUN

BEECRAIGS

Edinburgh

STENTON

LAMMERMUIR

DALKEITH

Motherwell

STRATHCLYDE
PARK

CLYDESDALE

COREHOUSE

Peebles

GLENTRESS

Galashiels

A84

Biggar

CARDRONA

ELIBANK

Kelso

Selkirk

BOWHILL

Jedburgh

Hawick

Moffat

CRAIK

WAUCHOPE

ENGLAND

Berw
o
Twe

ESKDALEMUIR

CASTLE O'ER

Lockerbie

Langholm

SOLWAY FIRTH

BORDER AREA

KEY: ♠ —RECREATIONAL FACILITIES
○ —TOWNS
SCALE: 1″ represents 10 miles

# The Borders and Lothian

The boundaries of this area I have arbitrarily selected as east of the A74 trunk road to an imaginary line from Clyde to Forth. Most of the state forests in this area have been planted since the last war and do not have very much visitor appeal. The private sector's forests are halved between the forest management companies with their very young plantations and a large range of estate woods from Buccleuch Estates at Selkirk and Dalkeith to the far-sighted farmer with his "twenty-acre" shelter belt. This area does not have a high area of forest, because it has for centuries been the centre of Scotland's sheep rearing industry, which created a grassland monoculture over the smooth terrain.

The underlying physical geography coupled with established sheep husbandry techniques are the dominant factors in the scenery. The parent bedrock has been clothed with substantial layers of glacial material upon which, depending on its structure, varying deposits of peat have accumulated. The whole peneplain has subsequently been eroded into a series of long valleys by rivers which mostly drain in a north to south direction. The largest of these rivers is the Tweed and it is in the upper reaches of this glen that my first selected forest lies.

# Glentress Forest

This large forest possesses some of the older Forestry Commission plantations in the area. It is now a large forest of around 10,000 hectares and is a management amalgamation of what was once six forests — Eddleston, Cardrona, Yair Hill, Dreva, Elibank and Traquair, and Glentress itself. Because of the climate and soil a variety of species was used, principally Spruce, Larch, Pine and Douglas Fir. The aesthetic value of the forest has been enhanced because windblow and the early replacement of the low yielding pines and larches by other more profitable species has created openings in the canopy and a bigger edge to plantation which in turn encourages more varied wildlife. You will see very good semi-mature Douglas fir in this forest and the forester's plans are that some of the best of these trees are going to be left to grow to a large size and on good ground this species will be continued to be used. The most important species used on the higher elevation plantings is Sitka Spruce.

The forest office and main visitor centre is situated on the A72 just two miles south of Peebles on the road to Galashiels. There you will find a tidy car park even though it is a working place with offices, store sheds, and workshops. The opportunity to picnic is provided by tables and chairs on the mown grass prettily situated under birch trees beside Glentress Burn. There are toilets but no facilities for the disabled.

**Information** This is provided by a small but excellent visitor centre with good displays by Peebles High School, some of whose senior pupils helped to lay out the walks. Useful information both about forest operations and the forest and its wildlife is given and there is a supply of free literature.

**Picnicking** Round the car park there are tables and benches of pleasing design with a small playground for children and an interesting group of tree sculptures overlooking the playground. These were done by forest staff using a chainsaw for the Forestry Commission Jubilee exhibition in 1967. They provide an interesting frontispiece for the walk leaflet. An attractive feature of the walks in this forest is the siting of small picnic sites along the length of the walk and I would recommend that you carry your picnic to one of these not too distant spots. There are a couple of tables just a quarter of a mile away on the yellow walk with a view over the Tweed valley. But do remember to take your litter home.

## Forest Walks

This is the main recreational activity within this forest and is availabe at three separate locations.

## Glentress

All the walks start at the car park where there is a large descriptive map and a box with free leaflets describing the walks and providing a scale map.

The walks are colour coded and waymarked by using a green painted stob (Scots word for fence post) with coloured incised rings and a white direction arrow cut into the top. At an intersection you should see two posts, one with the colour on the path to follow and the other with the remaining colours. The system is quite simple; but the problem of vandalism is everywhere, no less in the forest than in the city, so make sure that you check every post for the colour of your walk. If it is missing then you have missed your turn-off so retrace your steps until you see a road, path, or brashed lane leading off. The odds are that it will be your route, and you should soon come across a marker post. (*Note*: "brashed" is a forestry term for the removal of the dead bottom branches of a tree to allow access into the stand.)

The way-marking of forest walks is very difficult to do properly and standards vary with the individuals who set out the route. Walking through a forest is different from walking out in the open because the scale is hard to become accustomed to. You must look around at objects near at hand like the branches, bark, wildlife, and the forest floor and try not to look too far into the distance. If you do try always to look into the distance then you will experience a feeling of being lost, or rather, not knowing exactly where you are in relation to the external geography of your surroundings. You can overcome this by bringing your horizon and perspective within the compass of a few trees around you. The forester can help by laying out the waymarkers very carefully; but if you are confused, try to think your way out of the situation by pressing on and remembering exactly where you have been.

If you find that your selected walk has been closed by flooding or forest operations please obey the signs and choose an alternative. If you are on a walk where these obstacles are not brought to your attention prior to setting out then consult your map and try to find a route round the hazard. For example, if you are on a forest road quite high up a glen there will be another parallel road anything from 300 to 600 yards below you so strike straight off down the hill. If you do not have the confidence to do this then just simply retrace your steps. I have done this often and have been amazed at the things I missed on the way up.

The greatest enjoyment one gets from walking through a wood away from workaday pressures in the clean air comes from peace of mind. If the pitfalls are known then surely this increases the possibility of maximum enjoyment.

There are four walks: the *Yellow walk* is a pleasant short mile, and although it is just a little bit steep for the elderly or a baby in a pushchair, it is a comfortable walk for most people. It is ideal for those who want to stop for lunch then take a short walk to stretch their legs. There are no worthwhile trees to see, but there is a nice view out over the Tweed valley to the policies of Kalzie. the viewpoint is also a picnic spot so carry your lunch up for a table with a view. This walk can easily be done in reverse.

*Opposite: a typical forest trail through mature conifers.*

44

*The Orange walk* is another shortish walk, around two and a half miles. The path itself is not suitable for the elderly or babies as it climbs a path upwards from above the picnic site on the Yellow walk up through larch to a good viewpoint on a forest road. It continues up over the hill fort on Cardie Hill, to descend by mainly forest roads to the car park. The route passes some recently constructed ponds which are going to be a really beautiful feature when established. The originator is to be congratulated. Broadleaved trees have been planted round these two ponds and with the backdrop of good quality mature Douglas Fir this will be an excellent sylvan view.

If you cannot manage to go the whole walk but want to see the ponds, just reverse the colours you are following and carry on up the road with the red, blue, and orange circles as far as your time will allow. This walk, too, can be reversed which makes it a bit easier as the ascent is on road.

The *Blue Walk* is longer at four miles and can be tackled in either direction. My own preference is to leave the road as early as possible but I suggest you plan this walk round the use of the picnic place which is either three miles or four miles away. Although this is a pleasant walk it has too many miles of forest road for my liking. Forest roads are constructed primarily to carry timber lorries to the main public road. They are structurally very strong but lack a smooth surface so they make difficult walking at times. Even pushing a child's pushchair is hard work for the pusher, and wearing on both the occupant and the chair's construction. However, the roads are an easy way of finding your way round a forest so if you plan to spend a whole holiday near a forest where you intend to walk it will be worth your while buying an O.S. 1/50,000 map of the area as most forest roads are now shown. This will give you the freedom to make up your own walks, once you have gained some experience.

The *Red Walk* is the longest of the four at four and a half miles. Once again plan your route round the picnic site if you intend to use it. This walk is wholly on forest roads so while the views may be worthwhile my comments on the blue walk roads also apply here.

In addition to the walks at Glentress itself there are three walks at Cardrona which is about four miles from Peebles on the B7062. This road goes down the west bank of the Tweed so you have to cross the river in Peebles, turn left onto Kingsmeadows Road and follow it downstream.

There is a pleasant picnic site beside the Kirk Burn with three walks leading off: the *Orange Walk*, the shortest, at two miles, follows up the burn then returns through a youngish wood which has been thinned. This walk is not suitable for the elderly or for pushchairs. The *Yellow Walk* is a three-mile walk to Cardrona Castle, which the Forestry Commission is renovating. The *Red Walk* is a longer walk, of four miles, which is mainly on footpaths through the forest to a hill fort and a fine view of the Tweed and Peebles. There is even a seat for you to rest and enjoy the view. Then past Cardrona Castle and back to the car park.

All three walks are pleasant, a bit steep in places, through some young larch which nevertheless has been thinned so you do not get a shut in feeling. My only slight criticism is of the rustic handrails on the steeper parts. These degrade very quickly and become a bit of a nuisance.

## Cardrona Walks

This is a short walk of some one and a quarter miles through Yair Hill Plantation which is near Galashiels.

## Yair Hill Walk

All in all Glentress Forest is an ideal introduction to forest recreation as it is well looked after, near large centres and is in the drier half of the country so footwear should not be a problem. There is a good variety of tree species with some fine examples of Douglas Fir.

An interesting evening's walk can be enjoyed by walking up the Tweed from Peebles through Hay Lodge Park past Neidpath Castle. If you continue past the castle you enter some old mixed woodlands with some fine Beech and Scots Pine. A booklet is available from the information centre in Peebles.

## Neidpath Castle Walk

# Edinburgh and District

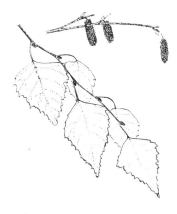

## The Royal Botanic Gardens

A visit to a large botanic garden is always worth while but to visit one which is older than Kew and which has an outstanding collection of conifers and rhododendrons which are all authoritatively labelled is surely a must for those interested in trees.

## Dalkeith Park

This is owned and run by Buccleuch Estates and is one of the Duke of Buccleuch and Queensberry's houses. There is a variety of walks through the policies with a guide book available from an information centre. There is also an adventure play area in a woodland setting, which is always guaranteed to appeal to all children from age ten upwards.

# Hopetoun House Nature Trail

This stately home in its splendid policies is situated near South Queensferry. There are signs on the M90 just before the Forth Road Bridge. A two mile walk which during the summer can be ranger guided with views over the Firth of Forth. There are all the recreational facilities associated with large open estates such as gift shop, restaurant, exhibits and picnic areas.

*A family share the enjoyment of a forest walk.*

# East Lothian and Berwickshire

The Forestry Commission provide some facilities in this predominantly agricultural area. These are:

*Monynut Picnic Site*, near the village of Innerwick, just off the A1.

*Pressmennan Forest Trail* starts near Stenton and provides a walk of two miles with views of the East Lothian countryside, some of the best agricultural land in Scotland.

*Danskine Loch*, near Gifford on the B6355 where a permit to fish for carp is available.

*Pease Bay Forest Walk*, on an unclassified road two miles east of Cockburnspath and just off the A1 there is a walk through broadleaves affording views of the sea.

# Borders

## Bowhill

Another of the Duke of Buccleuch's estates, this can be found three miles west of Selkirk on the A708, then follow signs. Buccleuch estates have always been one of the major forestry estates of Scotland so as well as an extensive and large policy wood there are considerable commercial plantations in the Yarrow and Ettrick valleys. During the summer the house with its wonderful art collection is open to the public. There is a gift shop and tearoom in a stable courtyard and another of the estate's exciting adventure playgrounds (more like a mini assault course). There is an information centre where a guide book can be bought.

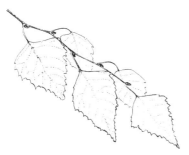

## Border Hill Forests

In three of the four border forests which belong to the Forestry Commission there are some walks and picnic places.

# Wauchope Forest

A picnic site known as *Piet's Nest* is situated four miles south of Bonchester Bridge on the B6357.

# Craik Forest

From a picnic site there are two forest walks. These are found up the Borthwick Water on the minor road to Craik which turns left off the B711 at Roberton. The walks are one and a half and three miles long with the longer going to Wolfcleuchhead waterfall where there are some seats. Pony trekking is available from a local farm but it would be best to check at the forest office first. If you are staying in the area it would be worth a visit for the whole day if the weather was fine and you were looking for a quiet peaceful day.

# Castle o'er Forest

There is a picnic site on the B723 road from Lockerbie to Eskdalemuir beside the Black Esk River.

# Eskdalemuir Forest

This is a large forest run by one of the forestry management companies called the Economic Forestry Group. It is a very young forest covering an area of twelve thousand hectares. Part of the group's service to the owners of the plantations is to manage and advise about land use, sporting, leisure and amenity developments. To this end at Eskdalemuir they have set up a commercial sporting and recreational enterprise which offers: roe deer stalking, rough shooting, driven grouse and pheasant shooting, duck flighting, fishing for trout on stocked ponds, a clay pigeon shooting range, pony trekking, wildlife photography, wildlife conservation studies, hill walking, weekly sporting parties, a forest centre (open by appointment), and holiday accommodation. Information from: Economic Forestry (Scotland) Ltd, Forestry House, Moffat, Dumfries.

# Corehouse Nature Reserve

There are two trails of about a mile to three miles through Clyde Valley Gorge with a variety of broadleaved species. The gorge is dry except for open days when the Electricity Board opens the dam. This facility is run by the Scottish Wildlife Trust and guide books and permission for certain areas can be had from 18 Ladyacre Road, Lanark. The reserve is situated at Kirkfieldbank on the A72, south of Lanark.

# Country Parks

In this central area there are two country parks run by local authorities worthy of mention. These are: *Strathclyde Country Park* which lies beside the River Clyde between Motherwell and Wishaw, and *Beecraigs Country Park* which is two miles south of Linlithgow on the minor roads linking that town with the M8. Although they are off the tourist routes both are important for the recreational facilities they provide for the local urban populations and both contain valuable pockets of trees in the largely industrial landscape.

# Clydesdale Forest

The forest provides two out of the way picnic sites at *Wilsontown* on the A706 and another at *Camilty* beside *Crosswoodburn* on the A70 sixteen miles south-east of Edinburgh.

SOUTH WEST

Greenock

FINLAYSTONE

CORNALEES

Glasgow

Largs

Paisley

MUIRSHILL

Kilmarnock

A74

Ayr

Cumnock

CULZEAN

Maybole

DRUMLANRIG

Girvan

Thornhill

CARRICK

AE

New Galloway

CLATTERINGSHAWS

Dumfries

GLENTROOL

BENNAN

MABIE

PENNINGHAME

KIRROUGHTREE

Stranraer

Newton Stewart

Castle Douglas

DALBEATTIE

CASTLE KENNEDY

FLEET

LOGAN GARDENS

BAREAGLE

SOLWAY FIRTH

KEY:   ◯ —TOWNS

↟ —RECREATIONAL FACILITIES

# Galloway and the South West

This area is bounded by the Firth of Clyde and A74 road to the north and east and the Solway Firth in the south. The geography of this area is rougher and wilder than the Borders; it is also wetter. The highest hill in the Southern Uplands, Merrick, is to be found here. It is 2764 feet (843 metres) above sea level. The geology in this area is one of glacial deposits overlying three distinct parent rocks. In the north of the area, the rocks are Carboniferous; in Renfrewshire Basalt; and in most of Ayrshire productive and unproductive coal measures. What could be termed the Galloway Foothills are of the Ordovician/Silurian series with hard shales and a rock called greywacke. Finally, in central Galloway intrusive granite can be found.

The southern half of this area is one of Scotland's most heavily forested regions with sixteen per cent of land in Dumfries and Galloway under trees. Most of these areas have been planted since 1950 but there are some older plantations such as at Solway Forest and on the Duke of Buccleuch's estate at Drumlanrig. The Forestry Commission owns sixty-five thousand hectares while the private owner has thirty-five thousand hectares. Most of the private plantations are very young and are under the management of the forestry companies. An example is Carsphain Forest with some five and a half thousand hectares planted in the early seventies. The Forestry Commission's largest holding is in the Galloway Forest Park which straddles the counties of Kirkcudbrightshire and South Ayrshire. Scenically the landscape patterns are still predominantly agricultural as forestry has more or less confined its activities to the uplands.

**Recreation** The countryside appears quieter than further north, perhaps because the area can absorb more people and cars since it is much better provided with roads. It is a diverse area with sparsely populated areas like upland Kirkcudbrightshire, and the busy seaside resorts and commuter towns of coastal Ayrshire. Forest recreation undoubtedly centres on the Galloway Forest Park.

# Galloway Forest Park

The Galloway Forest Park was thus designated in 1943, and consists of the following forests: Carrick, Clatteringshaws, Dundeugh, Bennan, Kirroughtree, and Glen Trool, making up an area of 63,000 hectares. The plantations are composed mainly of Sitka Spruce but there are large areas of Larch and in the peat bogs (of which there are quite a few), a mixture of Sitka and Lodgepole Pine was planted. The usual pattern is followed with most of the plantations being young; but at the Bennan there are some fifty year old compartments.

**The Queen's Way** The park is bisected by the A712 road, named the Queen's Way to commemorate the Silver Jubilee of Queen Elizabeth II. This was formally opened by H.R.H. Princess Anne during the summer of 1978. It is intended that along the length of this road from New Galloway to Newton Stewart landscaping and amenity will be the main management priority. Certainly along this route there is an impressive range of facilities. Travel from New Galloway towards Newton Stewart, and you will find them as follows:

**Bruce's Stone** This large stone which is about 600 yards off the road commemorates a battle fought by King Robert Bruce of Scotland against King Edward I of England in 1307 in the guerilla campaign he mounted early in the Wars of Scottish Independence. The actual stone and its immediate environs are owned by the National Trust for

Scotland but the Forestry Commission have constructed a car park and paths to the stone. The path is suitable for pushchairs.

A few hundred yards along the road is the Galloway Deer Museum. It is well signposted so you will not miss it. There is a large car park beside Clatteringshaws loch and a gravel path leading to the museum which has been sited in the steading of the house. Special arrangements can be made for the disabled to be driven to the door of the museum. The museum is very well appointed, and two special features are the collection of original bird paintings by local artist Donald Watson and the stained glass window which was specially commissioned by the Forestry Commission. It depicts local wildlife and was created by Brian Thomas OBE, who made the windows for Coventry Cathedral. The displays are of good local interest and well presented.

A stone near the entrance commemorates Princess Anne's opening of the Queen's Way. A path leads from here past a reconstructed Romano British Homestead to

## Galloway Deer Museum

*An interior view of the Galloway Deer Museum.*

Bruce's Stone. It is a good dry path suitable for pushchairs. Toilets with facilities for the disabled are available and the museum is open from April to September.

**The Raiders' Road**

This is the name given to a forest drive through the countryside Crockett used in his novel *The Raiders*. For a toll of 50p (1980) you can drive through mainly young plantations with riverside picnic places and another specially-commissioned piece of sculpture in the shape of an otter by Penny Wheatley. The pools are safe to splash about in. Keep a look-out for labels marking the different tree species. Near the end of the drive there is a scenic car park beside Stroan Loch where, if you are fortunate with your timing, you may see a hen harrier hunting. Two walks are waymarked — a short three quarters of a mile through pine and spruce, and a longer one and a quarter miles which climbs to the top of Bennan Hill where there are some dramatic views of the Ken valley. The viaduct to the south carried the now closed Stranraer to Dumfries railway. The trees on the hill to the north are forty-year-old Corsican Pine. The route continues through some high quality timber which is fifty-year-old Sitka Spruce. Note the volume of wood compared to the pine. When you reach the main road I suggest you turn left and drive up the side of Loch Ken to New Galloway as fine old Douglas Fir can be seen growing on the hill on your left. If you turn right it will eventually take you to Laurieston where you can either go to Castle Douglas or on to the main A75.

**Red Deer Range**

This is a large enclosure on the hill called Brockloch to the north of the Queen's Way. For the casual visitor there is a car park and a path up to a viewpoint where if you are lucky you may see some deer. I was there in the rut when the stags vocally fight for the possession of the females or hinds so I was lucky enough to hear and see some. To make sure of a better chance to see them you will have to be there at either dawn or dusk. Better still if you are really keen, make arrangements with the forester at Clatteringshaws forest office to use, for a fee, the hide.

Farther on past Craigdews bridge there is the goat park where a small herd of wild Galloway goats have been enclosed. As goats become tame over the years this is a good place to take young children as they will definitely see goats near the west end at Murray's monument.

**Goat Park**

Near the middle of the goat park a ruined cottage on the opposite side of the road is signposted as "Murray's Birthplace." This is the birthplace of a shepherd's son who by the time of his early death at the age of 37, had become Professor of Oriental languages at Edinburgh University. The Forestry Commission used their own drystone dyker to partly reconstruct the ruin in commemoration of a worthy achievement. The obelisk which immediately draws your eye, standing as it does on that steep little knowe, also commemorates Alexander Murray.

**Murray's Birthplace**

This campsite is splendidly situated at the centre of the Queen's Way and its range of facilities. It is attractively sited on the banks of the Palnure Burn. The bare rocky crags of Craigdews and Craignelder stand to the east, where you may be lucky enough to see the lazy circling of the Golden Eagle. To the west is Murray's Monument on its little hill with the plantations of Kirroughtree Forest rising above it. The burn is safe to splash in, and just below the site is a pool where the more experienced can swim.

**Talnotry Campsite**

I must admit that I like Talnotry for its situation and size — about a hundred units. It is a Class B site, open from Easter until the end of September. Bookings for more than three nights will be accepted. Remember that you must have your own toilet facilities or you will not be allowed in. There are minimum facilities — stand pipes for water; a hard ring access road; chemical toilet disposal points; and a non-resident warden who runs a small shop for milk and day-to-day requirements. Newton Stewart, the nearest town with a full range of shops, is only about eight miles away. Forest facilities within walking distance are: Murray's Monument, Murray's Birthplace, the Goat Park, a forest trail, and the Grey Mare's Tail Waterfalls. In addition, you may fish in the Black Loch — permits may be obtained from the warden of this loch, which is stocked with brown trout and is for fly fishing only until the end of June. Facilities a little farther away are: The Raider's Road, the Red Deer Range, the Galloway Deer Museum, Kirroughtree Forest — with its information centre, picnic sites, arboretum, and a forest trail (see Kirroughtree Forest). There is also fishing in Lilie's Loch and Loch of the Lowes and Loch Dee. A leaflet giving the latest information will be available from the warden but briefly all three are stocked with brown trout and permits are available either at the site shop or the Deer Museum.

## Talnotry Forest Trail

This starts in the woods just across the road from the campsite entrance. Booklets which are essential are available from the camp shop or other Forestry Commission offices for a bargain 15 pence. The walk, which is steep and rough in places, encompasses viewpoints, waterfalls, old mine workings, and goes some way along a forest road which is built on top of the old Edinburgh road. This was probably the old pilgrim route from the capital to the holy shrines at Whithorn, where St Ninian started his missionary work. The Countryside Commission for Scotland is planning to open a long-distance walkway from Portpatrick to Dunbar, and it will surely follow this road.

The route is four miles long and it is suggested that it will take about two and a half hours. It is not recommended for the elderly or very young children. The booklet, which I must stress is essential, follows the standard format for trails in Galloway and is easily followed. It has attractive scraper-board drawings and informative text about everything you are likely to see. The map though sketchy has all the salient points needed to help you along. A good feature is the provision of two short-cuts which enable you to vary the walk. *Boots or wellingtons must be worn.*

Two attractive well-kept picnic sites are available in this section of the Queen's Way. Both are easily accessible from the road with the latter providing a nice viewpoint.

**Talnotry and Glen of the Bar Picnic Sites**

Round the forest office at Daltamie can be found another cluster of facilities. On the A75 about four miles from the A712 junction there is a sign directing you to Kirroughtree Forest.

**Kirroughtree Forest**

There are about sixty different broadleaved and coniferous species, all properly labelled and with a brief description. A half-mile waymarked path takes you round the arboretum. Wellingtons should be worn except in dry weather.

**Forest Garden**

A well-maintained sunny spot, but be prepared for breezes.

**Daltamie Picnic Place**

A small information centre is situated in one of the steading buildings. It is primarily intended for the children from the nearby education centre but everyone is welcome. It contains mostly forestry information.

**Information Centre**

The booklet available from most Forestry Commission offices in Galloway is essential for this four-mile trail. The booklet is pretty, with a wealth of information about forestry aimed, I suspect, at school children; but it is quite difficult to follow and relate to the route. I found the signposting unhelpful, but the area had recently been logged so perhaps a few of the signs were missing. Part of the path had been used as a skidder route so was difficult to walk on and it was not possible to walk at the side because of the brash. There are two shortened trails within the four miles so a short walk of about an hour can be taken. The nursery is now no longer in production so some of the information is dated. If you want forestry information, however, a visit to garden, information centre and a leisurely completion of the trail is the best introduction available.

**Larg Hill and Bruntis Forest Trail**

# Glen Trool Forest

This very large forest of around 13,000 hectares of plantation also has 10,000 hectares of hill tops and other unplantable areas. It is a young forest of mainly Sitka Spruce but with considerable areas of pine and larch. It also has some important remnants of oak woods within its area. It, too, has a large range of recreational facilities.

**Holiday Houses** There are fourteen semi-detached houses available in Glen Trool forest village. These were built to house forest workers but are now no longer needed. They are fully furnished with a cooker and fridge and can sleep five. Details and booking forms can only be had through Forestry Commission headquarters in Edinburgh (see page 36 for address). I think they are quite attractive for a holiday provided you have a car and expect to use it to go about as there is very little to do there without one.

**Caldons Campsite** This is a large Class A campsite situated at the south-west end of Loch Trool. It is open from 1 April until 30 September and advance bookings can be taken although there are no marked pitches. The site is supervised by a resident warden who runs a shop which has most day to day needs and at present a milkman calls. For other requirements there is a shop at Glentrool village, three miles away, or the nearest town — Newton Stewart — is thirteen miles away, and has a large range of shops. There is space for 250 tents or caravans, and other facilities include flush toilets, wash rooms and showers with free hot water, electric shaver points, washing and drying facilities and a recreation hut.

The site is spread through an open birch, oak, alder wood and campers are free to choose their own sites under the trees or by the side of Caldons Burn. There is a variety of things to do from the site. Walking is catered for by three marked routes:

## Loch Trool Trail

This walk of some four and a half miles is of considerable botanical interest as it goes through three distinct broadleaved woods which have been designated "Sites of Special Scientific Interest" (SSSI) by the Nature Conservancy Council. These are thought to be remnants of the indigenous broadleaved forest which covered most of southern Scotland up until the time of the Normans. Historic interest is provided by crossing one of Bruce's battlegrounds at the Steps of Trool and passing a memorial stone known as Bruce's Stone.

There is a booklet about the trail, which is not essential, although I would urge you to buy it as it is full of information both about the forest and its historical connections, is well produced and would make an interesting souvenir.

Remember you are in the wet part of the country so expect a path to be wet and muddy and wear your boots. Do also remember that you can cause fires by careless action, especially in the spring.

## Jenny's Hill Walk

A short waymarked walk up the Caldons Burn to Jenny's Hill for views of the surrounding countryside. A fine walk on a summer's night. It is about two and a half miles, and do wear boots.

## Martyr's Tomb

A short quarter-mile walk to a Covenanter's memorial tomb through the oak woods of Coldons Wood which is a "SSSI."

## Stroan Bridge Walk

This walk is a link with the other forest trails situated at Stroan Bridge some two and a half miles away. Unless you are very keen and fit I think the five miles there and back plus the three and a half miles of the trail will be too much for most people. However, there is a nice walk along the bank of the Water of Trool so if you can arrange a lift in a car there or back it would be worth considering.

## Merrick Walk

This is a waymarked hill-climb so you must be properly equipped and have the necessary experience and degree of physical fitness to undertake a walk of this nature. Merrick is the highest hill in southern Scotland at 843 metres (2764 feet). The path starts from Bruce's Stone car park, climbs up the Buchan Burn, past a ruined cottage known as Culsharg on to the shoulder known as Benyellary. A high level walk with fine views into the wilderness area beyond takes you to the top, having travelled a map distance of about three and a half miles. Unless you have previous experience of climbing you must follow the signposts back. Do not be tempted to try another route as there are cliffs all around you.

## Wilderness Area

For those climbers and ramblers who want to find the true peace of mind that comes from the challenge of walking in a true wilderness, then the area northwards from Loch Dee to Loch Macaterick takes in about forty square miles of wonderful hill land studded with more than a dozen lochs and lochans. I do not share a viewpoint currently fashionable among climbers that these areas should not be publicised as they then would become too popular and lose the magic status of "wilderness." If you are fit and experienced enough to plan and execute an expedition to them you will be sensible enough to treat them as something special and fragile and not spoil their sensitive environment by brash destructive action or behaviour. I must emphasise that you must be very fit, be properly equipped with good boots, map, compass, survival gear, the knowledge of how to use them, and an awareness of the mountain safety code. You must leave details of your route in your car or with the camp warden and your estimated time and place of your arrival back. Finally, you must take extreme care not to start a fire.

To help you enjoy a foray into this area the Forestry Commission have allowed the Mountain Bothies Association to take over the upkeep of five bothies (rough shelters). They are: *Tunskeen*, NX 424906; *White Laggan*, NX 467774; *Back Hills o' Bush*, NX 481843; *Shiel of Castlemaddy*, NX 578901; and *Cross Burn*, NX 375878. Please look after them and remember to leave no trace of your stay there.

## Bruce's Stone Car Park

A large car park near a memorial cairn to Bruce where you can enjoy splendid views of Loch Trool and surrounding hills. A small craft shop is open during the

summer, run by ladies from nearby Glen Trool Village. The feral goats come to be fed so keep an eye on your picnic.

*Bruce's Stone, Glen Trool Forest Park.*

## Stroan Bridge

A large car park with toilets run by the District Council is situated beside The Water of Minnoch which conveniently goes over a waterfall at this point. The Forestry Commission Stroan Bridge Trail is an informative trail over a maximum of three and a half miles (there are shorter loops within). Where the Loch Trool trail centred on the historical aspects, this one gives forestry information. It can be wet, so wear wellingtons unless you are there during a dry spell. A booklet is available from the forest offices or campsite shop. There are plenty of attractive picnic tables set out alongside the burn. The waters can be dangerous, so watch the children.

*Youth Campsites* are available in this forest. Enquiries to: Recreation Forester, Glentrool Forest Office, Bargrennan, Newton Stewart. *Tel* Bargrennan 200.

**Fishing** The Water of Minnoch can be fished from Kirriereoch to its source for salmon and trout during August and September. Permits, restricted to six per day are available from Caldons Campsite.

**White Cairn Walk** This short walk of one and a half miles starts from Glentrool village, goes through young plantations to a "Chambered Tomb" which gives the walk its name.

**Picnicking** There are, in addition five other simple picnic sites with a few tables and a guiding signpost. Three are on the unclassified road from Bargennan to Straiton, one is on the A714 Newton Stewart to Girvan road, while one is on the unclassified road from Stroan Bridge to Minnigaff. On windless days I would recommend using any of the three on the Straiton road as fine views of the hills can be had. When the wind is blowing try Larg picnic place on the Minnigaff road which is in a broadleaved setting.

**Signposting** All of the facilities in the Glentrool park are of a very high standard and you will have no trouble finding them. I was particularly pleased to see advance warning notices of the facility on the public roads.

# Carrick Forest

The main recreational activity in this forest is fishing which takes place in the hill lochs at the eastern end of the forest. This forest is near to the large population of coastal Ayrshire so the fishing is correspondingly busy. To avoid disappointment then, book ahead by writing or telephoning to: Mr R. Heaney, Talaminnoch, Straiton, *Tel* Straiton 617, *or* Forestry Commission, Carrick Forest, Barr, *Tel* Straiton 223.

The available fishings are:

*Loch Bradan*, five boats available for fly fishing on loch stocked with brown trout.

*Loch Skelloch*, one boat available on small hill loch.

*River Stinchar* About three miles of this fairly big river available for trout and salmon fishing. From Pincally to Linfern Burn.

*Breckbowie Loch*, one boat available on this small hill loch for fly fishing only.

*Dhu Loch* Fly fishing only available on this small loch deep in the forest.

*Linfern Loch* Pike fishing on this hill loch.

## Walks

There are two long walks of about six miles length which start from Stinchar car park, eight miles from Straiton on the Straiton to Bargrennan road. *Cornish Hill Walk* which takes you on to fine high, craggy country with excellent views. *Stinchar Falls Walk* is along the banks of the River Stinchar and should be undertaken, if possible, after heavy rain when the falls are spectacular. Take a picnic and enjoy the views from a well-positioned seat while eating.

## Picnic Sites

*Changue*, situated in attractive mixed woodland about three-quarters of a mile from Barr on the B734.

*Tairlaw Toll* situated in young conifers on the Straiton to Bargrennan road has a burn; there is a children's play area.

# Dundeugh Forest

The forest offers fishing on the Polmaddie Burn. Both banks are available from the forest office to Forest Lane, then the north bank only to the Shiel of Castlemaddie. Permits are available from the forest office which is just off the A713 about six miles north of Dalry. With nine or ten miles of burn available, they surely offer value for distance.

We now move out of Galloway Forest Park in a westwards direction to Culzean.

# Culzean Country Park

There are walks and policy woods, cliffs, sandy coves, ponds, gardens, a large impressive castle once belonging to the Stewarts, restaurants, displays, warden service, talks and films, and plenty of places to picnic. The park is run by the National Trust for Scotland for the local authorities and can be found on the A719, twelve miles south of Ayr.

## Castle Kennedy Gardens

On the A75 some four miles east of Stranraer, the gardens are worth a visit to see a fine avenue of monkey puzzle trees (*Araucaria araucana*) which come from South America, and in May to see the avenue of Chilean fire tree (*Embothrium* spp.). In addition there are many fine woods and gardens, a ruined castle and a fine mansion house. The estate belongs to the Earl of Stair.

# Logan Gardens

On the A716 Sranraer to Drummore road, Logan has a fine collection of semi-tropical trees and shrubs. It is an annexe to the Royal Botanic Gardens in Edinburgh.

# Bareagle Forest

A walk through one of the few young oak plantations the Forestry Commission possesses in Scotland. The walk is at a place caled Hazelbank on the A746, about a mile from Sorbie. The oak and the larch were planted at about the same time in a mixture and the plan is to remove the larch as thinnings when they mature and leave the oak to grow on. Notice then how long it takes an oak wood to be worthwhile.

# Fleet Forest

On the A75 at Gatehouse of Fleet this forest has a fine car park and picnic site under mature broadleaves from where there are three walks laid out.

**The Burn Walk**

This is a short walk of about a mile through managed broadleaved woodlands, and through the forest nursery where many thousands of young trees are raised annually.

**The Mote Walk**

A walk of about one and a half miles taken through the same woods to a Norman Mote.

**The Coronation Walk**

At three miles the longest walk, the route takes you past a folly known as "The Temple" and through woodland specially planted to commemorate the Coronation of King George VI in 1938.

All the walks are pleasant and I can recommend them. In wet weather the paths can be a bit muddy so wear boots.

**The Murray Forest Centre**  This is situated at the car park where there are simple displays of forest operations. A nice touch was the pots of young trees growing inside. The centre was presented to the Commission by Mrs Murray-Usher of Cally in 1969.

**Laurieston Picnic Site and Walk**  A pleasant site has been laid out on the B795 about one and a half miles from Laurieston village, which in itself is a fine drive over a hill road. A short walk of about a mile has been laid out through the young surrounding plantations.

# Threave Gardens

A National Trust property on the A75 about a mile west of Castle Douglas where there is a fine garden, an excellent information centre, and a woodland walk.

# Solway Forest

**Plantain Loch Forest Walks**  Start from a splendid picnic site on the A710 just on the outskirts of Dalbeattie. The site is situated under mature Douglas Fir nearly sixty years old and there are many high granite boulders and outcrops for the older child to use as a natural adventure playground. There are three walks in all, more or less based on the old granite-quarriers' paths.

*Craigmath Walk* is about a mile long. *Lochside Walk* is two miles long through mature conifer plantations round the loch where there are seats. *Quarry Walk* at three miles is to one of the old quarries and then rejoins the other walks. The paths have all been well set out with a high standard of signposting. I was there after very heavy rain when the path had been submerged by the loch flooding but I still managed to complete the walk in ordinary shoes. A pushchair could with difficulty be taken round the walk.

## Mabie Walks and Picnic Site

One and a half miles from Islesteps on the A710 can be found the signs leading to this well laid out picnic site with toilets and wet weather shelter. A booklet for the three walks is available from an honesty box. The booklet is essential so make sure you get one by visiting one of the Commission's offices just in case the box is empty. There are four walks which start in this interesting old policy wood where there are unusual specimen trees from Japan. All the trees have been labelled. Across the burn a larch seed orchard has been planted and is fully explained in the booklet. The four walks are respectively one, two, three and four miles long through varied plantations and with excellent viewpoints over the Nith estuary.

## Pony Trekking

This can be arranged in the forest through local stables, if interested enquire at Commission offices in the area.

## Shambellie Pinewoods

As you drive along the A710 you should notice some beautiful plantations of mature Scots Pine a mile north of New Abbey. There is an information notice.

# Ae Forest

The signs leading you to this excellent riverside picnic area can be found on the unclassified road from Ae village. The site itself is about one and a half miles into the forest and gives you the opportunity of viewing some magnificent stands of Norway spruce about forty years old. There is a spaciousness about the site which appealed to me. Two short walks of just over a mile are waymarked and I would recommend them if you want to see fine stands of managed Spruce trees. A leaflet is available from the forest office at Ae village. I really enjoyed my visit to Ae.

# Drumlanrig Castle

This is another of the Duke of Buccleuch's properties which has magnificent policy woods and gardens through which you can walk after visiting the castle. This estate, too, has an adventure playground, guaranteed to excite the older child. The estate can be found on the A76 some four miles north of Thornhill.

In the very north of this area as one nears the Clyde conurbation there are many fine waymarked walks in country and city parks where one can find a lot of arboricultural information. The most notable are:

*Strathclyde Park*, beside M74 between Motherwell and Hamilton.

*Muirshiel Country Park*, three miles north of Lochwinnoch on the B786.

*Cornalees Bridge Nature Trail*, three miles above Inverkip on the unclassified road to Greenock past Loch Thom.

*Finlaystone Woodland Walks*, about two miles past Langbank on the A8.

*Glasgow Parks*, visit the information centre in George Square for full information but to relieve the tedium of shopping I recommend a visit to Pollock Park where there are mature stands of broadleaves.

*Opposite: Red deer hind, browsing on oak saplings.*

# CENTRAL AREA

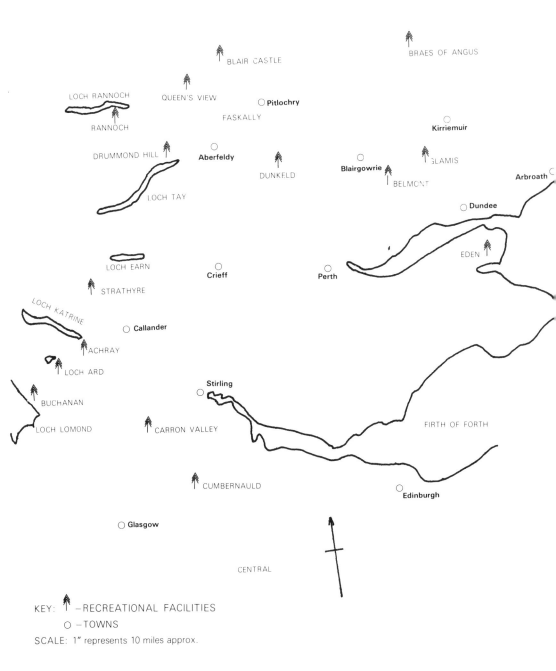

KEY: ♠ –RECREATIONAL FACILITIES
      O –TOWNS

SCALE: 1″ represents 10 miles approx.

# Central Scotland

I have arbitrarily fixed the boundaries of this area as the countryside east from Loch Lomondside and the A82, north from the line of the now closed Forth and Clyde Canal, south of a line from Kingshouse on Rannoch Moor to Montrose.

It is a very diverse area. Geographically it covers Highland and Lowland, landforms with forestry, agriculture, and heavy industry are all represented. It also stands immediately to the north of the most heavily concentrated urban area of Scotland. Since Victorian times and the growth of affluence it has always had an important recreational role. As the area is not homogeneous I do not intend attempting to describe it generally but plan to take you on an itinerary starting at Glasgow, going eastwards through Fife, north through Perthshire and Angus, then south to the Trossachs.


# Carron Valley Forest

This forest lies in the middle of the Lennox Hills just fifteen miles north of Glasgow. The hills are smooth peat covered basalt flows which are a feature of the central valley of Scotland. The forest area includes the second highest hill of the Lennox Range, Meikle Bin, which is 1870 feet (570 metres) above sea-level. It is a young forest of spruce with no outstanding scenic value except as a lung for the industrial towns to the south. The Forestry Commission has set down two picnic places at favourite spots.

75

**Spittal Bridge Picnic Place and Walks**  This is located on the B818 just a mile from where the Tak Ma Doon Road from Kilsyth joins it. There is safe paddling and three short waymarked walks are available of three-quarters, one and a half and three miles long.

**Sir John de Graham's Picnic Site**  This can be found at the west end of Loch Carron a quarter mile up an unclassified road to the north.

**Palacerigg Country Park**  This is primarily a wildlife orientated park but if you are travelling northwards through Glasgow it would be a convenient stop-over away from the busy roads. It can be found on an unclassified road leading from the B8054 south east of Cumbernauld.

# Eden Forest

This forest is situated in the agricultural area of the Howe of Fife and on the dune area of Tentsmuir North of St Andrews — a popular holiday town famous for its University and golf courses. There are various forest facilities available:

**Holiday House**  Threequarters of a mile away from Kinshaldy Beach the Forestry Commission has a holiday house available which sleeps six and is available all year. St Andrews is only eight miles away.

**Kinshaldy Beach**  This is a large extensive beach area immediately to the east of Tentsmuir Forest where there is a large car park, picnic area, play area, toilets and a small shop open during good weather in the holiday season. In addition there is a toilet for disabled people and a specially reserved car park for them on the beach. A small charge is levied for parking. It can be found by taking the B945 which is off the A92 Leuchars to Dundee road for about three miles then following the signs for Kinshaldy. This

76

is a pine forest with all three major commercial pine species present.

This can be found a quarter of a mile west of the A914 about two miles before its junction with the A91 near the village of Ladyburn. There you will find a picnic area with a large grassy play area beneath tall pine trees. There are toilets, including one for the disabled and two nice and easy waymarked walks of about a half and one mile long through open pinewoods.

**Edensmuir Picnic Place and Walks**

# Perth

If you stop any time in Perth there are a number of woods to visit.

This is a local authority walk on Kinnoull Hill on the outskirts of Perth. There is a small charge for parking and a guide book is available. The walk is through deciduous woodlands to a viewpoint at the top of the hill. It can be found on the A85.

**Kinnoull Hill Trail**

# Dunkeld Forest

The Forestry Commission has a waymarked walk on the unclassified road from Perth to Kinfauns. There is a car park, toilets (including one for the disabled) and an easy walk of about one and a quarter miles which links up with the Kinnoull Hill walks. Panoramic views of the Tay Estuary can be had after walking through mixed woods of beech and pines.

**Jubilee Walks**

On the way to Braes of Angus Forest and our next major stop three places are worth a mention:

The Palace is open to the public, and some fine trees can be seen in the policies.

**Scone Palace**

**Meiklour Beech Hedge**

On the road to Blairgowrie a row of very fastigiate beech trees have grown into a hedge over a hundred feet high — worth seeing.

**Belmont Estate Nature Trail**

The trail is on the A927 a mile south of Meigle, laid out by Dundee District Council with a booklet, car park and play area. There are fine views of Strathmore and the Highlands beyond as you walk through this estate with its parks and woods.

# Braes of Angus Forest

For the first time we now cross the Highland Fault and enter the mountains in this our turning point for our journey round this area. To find the facilities in this forest take the B955 from Kirriemuir to Clova then the unclassified road for the remaining four miles to Glen Doll Lodge which is now a Youth Hostel. There is a car park and picnic place for which there is a small charge, with toilets (including one for the disabled). Several short walks have been waymarked with good views of the mountains and glen. Pony Trekking can be arranged through local riding stables (Contact: Forestry Commission, Dykehead, Cortachy, Kirriemuir; *Tel* Cortachy 204).

This is available for the experienced walker who intends to traverse the long distance hill route to Ballater and Braemar. These famous routes are "Jock's Road" which is fourteen miles long and climbs to a height of 3143 feet (958 metres). The Capel track at fifteen miles climbs over the Capel Mountain to Loch Muick and then on to Ballater. Another, south-eastwards to Glen Isla, is the longest at eighteen miles. These are mountain tracks and all the usual mountaineering precautions should be taken.

## Backpacking Campsite

1. Have good equipment and know how to use it.
2. Leave details of your intended route and estimated time and place of arrival.
3. Carry emergency food and shelter.
4. The winter conditions are severe — you should be equipped for these and know how to use your equipment.

The whole area is a great centre for a mountain walking holiday with magnificent scenery. Definitely a must for the enthusiast.

We must now travel east to visit Dunkeld where so many of our modern plantation forestry techniques were pioneered by various Dukes of Atholl. Strathmore has always been important both as a route and a strategic military position, standing as it does at the edge of the Highlands. There are many castles, some of which are open to the public. In the policies you may see large individual specimens of exotic trees. Glamis, a National Trust property just off the A94 about five miles east of Forfar, is a notable example. Round Dunkeld two properties are open to the public:

## Loch of Lowes

Off A923, two miles east of Dunkeld. This is primarily a wildlife reserve under the management of the Scottish Wildlife Trust (address on page 20) where there is a fully equipped observation hide. The main wildlife interest is in the nesting water birds and Ospreys. A handbook is available and the ecology of the area is demonstrated at the visitor centre. There is a ranger service:
*Tel* Dunkeld 337, *or* Ballinluig 267.

79

**Hermitage Forest Woodland Trail**

This property can be found on the B898, two miles west of Dunkeld on the Sma' Glen road to Crieff. It is managed by the National Trust for Scotland. There is a small charge for parking, a booklet is available, and ranger services are provided at Killiecrankie Visitor Centre (*Tel* Killiecrankie 233 and Ballinluig 324). The Hermitage path is beside the River Braan and contains many old, large specimens of Douglas fir and European larch. It passes a picturesque folly from which the walk is named.

While in Dunkeld another historic forestry site to visit is Dunkeld Cathedral where some of the earliest introduced European larch can be seen. The first Hybrid larch trees were discovered nearby.

The journey is now northwards past some outstanding forest scenery. There are the beautiful larch plantations of Atholl Estates on your right while the Forestry Commission plantations are across the Tay.

# Tummel Forest

**Faskally Picnic Site and Forest Walk**

This is situated in the policies of Faskally House which were once managed to retain their uneven age and mixture of species. The turn-off is just a mile north of Pitlochry. There is a car park and picnic site with toilets and a booklet is available from the Forest Centre at Queen's View or from the Tourist Centre in Pitlochry.

The walks are pleasant with the chance to see red squirrels if you are quiet. The opportunity exists to do these walks from Pitlochry. You should make your way to the Greenpark Hotel where the path commences.

**Queen's View**

This famous viewpoint with its westward view of Loch Tummel with Schiehallion in the background can be found on the B8019 road to Kinloch Rannoch about five miles from its junction with the A9. Queen Victoria viewed the loch from this point on one of her Highland jaunts, but it was already named Queen's View at that time.

The Forestry Commission has a large surfaced car park, toilets (with facilities for the disabled), a picnic area, a visitor centre, and a pleasant little walk up to the viewpoint with its indicator board and rail to lean on. It is quite a spectacular view best viewed, I think, at sunset as for me it is too busy during a fine summer day.

The *Visitor Centre*, open from April to September, has an information desk, exhibits, and a slide programme of the forest in Glen Garry, Glen Tummel and Glen Rannoch. There is a small entrance fee for adults. The opportunity exists for you to buy booklets of the various forest walks in the area as well as some of the excellent Forestry Commission literature on forest related subjects like wildlife. An additional attraction during June to September is a guided walk by a Forestry Commission Ranger. Walks start at two p.m. on Wednesdays and Sundays and leave from the centre.

## Allean Walks and Picnic Place

These can be found a quarter of a mile on from Queen's View. There is a system of walks on the side of the forested hill above Loch Tummel — good views but it can be steep and rough. A partially excavated ring fort and a reconstructed clachan are on the route. Walks range from one and three quarters to three miles.

## Killiecrankie

This property, managed by the National Trust, is the narrow, wooded gorge of the River Garry two miles north of Pitlochry just beyond Faskally. It was the site of a bloody battle between the Jacobites and the English in 1689. There is a very impressive visitor centre from which guided walks start in the summer. There is a series of walks, some quite stiff, through the broadleaved woods clothing the steep gorge slopes. The river is outstanding in spate.

## Blair Castle

The home of the Duke of Atholl, the policies of this impressive castle contain some magnificent specimens of our major commercial conifer species as befits an estate which has had a consistent forest policy for about two hundred years. Situated in Blair Atholl on the A9.

81

# Rannoch Forest

Travel westwards on the B8019 along the north shore of Loch Tummel. The birchwoods hereabouts are particularly fine as they are growing in something approaching their optimum environment. Turn left in Kinloch Rannoch and follow signs to the Forestry Commission campsite, some four miles along the south shore of Loch Rannoch.

**Kilvrecht Campsite** This is a class B campsite in a large clearing in a birch wood beside the Carie Burn and half a mile from the loch. It has 140 pitches for both tents and caravans. It is open from the end of March until the end of September. There are no advance booking facilities but enquiries should be made to the Forestry Commission, Kinloch Rannoch, Tayside, *Tel* Kinloch Rannoch 360.

**Fishing** Fishing (for brown trout) and boating are available on the loch. Permits from the camp warden.

**Forest Walks** These start at the site and range from one to five miles long through the birch and pine woods overlooking Loch Rannoch. The pinewoods of the Black Wood of Rannoch are a remnant of the old Caledonian Forest (see section on Scots Pine) and are being specially managed by the Forestry Commission to preserve and expand the wood, using existing parent stock.

**Picnic Sites** There are three small spots on the roadside towards Kinloch Rannoch.

**Holiday Houses** *East Camghouran* (NN 555562), equipped to high standard with electric cooker, fridge, water heater (electricity charges by 10p slot meter). This stone built cottage is set in a beautiful, if remote, part of the Highlands and is perfect for those whose interests lie in mountain walking, fishing, climbing, and getting away from it all for some refreshing peace and solitude. To help the mood, logs are available for meditative evenings beside the fire.

A waymarked path through the forest leads to the right of way over *Lairg Chalbhath* into Glen Lyon at Innerwick. This is about fourteen miles so you will either need a car to meet you or make other arrangements such as a bivouac. This is a mountain walk and should only be undertaken by the experienced who have followed the Mountain Code. There are innumerable interesting walks in this area for the fit and experienced. Examples are: Rannoch Station to Glencoe via Black Corries; to Loch Ossian where important forestry experiments took place at the beginning of this century; to Ben Alder Cottage (looked after by the Mountain Bothies Association) near a cave used by the fugitive Prince Charlie. For most of these walks you will have to be prepared to bivouac or use a bothy.

**Mountain Paths**

In this area you are in the middle of a large population of deer herds so you should have no problem in seeing and observing them. Remember, however, that every place in this small country of ours is managed by someone for a specific purpose. The deer, no matter how wild and inaccessible the place, are being managed and actually belong to someone who wants to stalk and shoot them for either sport or venison. You should be especially careful during August and September, the peak months for stag stalking. Middle to late October is a good time for seeing deer, as the rut is usually still in progress then and the stags are noticeable by the noise they make.

**Red Deer Watching**

# Drummond Hill Forest

This attractive older forest with good quality larch stands has some appealing walks at *The Mains* just a quarter of a mile north of *Kenmore* on the unclassified road to Coshieville. There is parking and a series of walks from two and a half to four miles long, and an excellent viewpoint over Loch Tay, Kenmore and Taymouth Castle, home of the Campbells of Breadalbane.

**Pony Trekking**    This can be arranged through local stables. Contact the Forestry Commission, *Dalerb*, Kenmore, Aberfeldy, *Tel* Kenmore 210.

**Picnicking**    At Balerb Picnic Place is a large grassy area between the loch and some larch woods. There is a small charge for parking but there are toilets (including facilities for the disabled) and a play area for children. Located about a mile from Kenmore on the road to Killin (A827).

In this locality there are some three other places worth looking at. There is a pleasant evening walk through the Birks of Aberfeldy, which starts in the town. The oldest tree in Europe, it is claimed, can be seen in Fortingall Churchyard. The tree, some three thousand years old, is now somewhat disappointing—a Yew with its centre gone and other age and vandal damage. There are many fine trees in Taymouth Castle policies.

84

# Strathyre Forest

This is a very spread-out forest so I suggest we approach this time from the east. A stop-over in Crieff can be turned to advantage by walking the trail through pleasant mixed woods. A booklet and details are available from the Information Centre in Crieff.

**Forest Walks**

*Craigmhor Walk.* This walk is primarily for users of the campsite at Milton, one mile east of Comrie on the A85 as no car parking is available. It is half a mile to the viewpoint over Comrie to Glen Artney.

*Devil's Cauldron Walk.* This circular two-mile walk starts at the edge of Comrie Golf Course and once again is limited to pedestrians as there is no car park. This walk leads up through mixed plantations (look out for the stand of *Abies Procera*) to a waterfall on the River Lednock. Deviate if you have a sense of direction and can ford the burn, and climb up to the Melville Monument for a marvellous view. Return by a path through pleasant mixed broadleaves with some nice beech and a resident population of grey squirrels. Remember this is private property so do no damage.

The local authority has signposted a series of walks through the wooded gorge of the River Lednock.

*Glen Tarken Walk.* A short walk through old oakwoods with views of Loch Earn. Parking is readily available on the side of the road (A85) due west of St Fillans.

**Strathyre Centre**

In "Bonnie Strathyre" the Forestry Commission has a large car park and a visitor centre with its display theme the recreational facilities offered by the Commission. The centre has been specially designed to accommodate wheelchairs.

Strathyre is very beautiful with steep conifer-clad mountains rising straight from Loch Lubnaig. It is close to the populous Central Valley and on one of the principal routes to the Highlands, and therefore is very busy, especially on public holidays.

There are two walks from the Centre car park — one is

an interpretative trail about one and a half miles long for which the explanatory leaflet is essential. The other is a longer hill climb to the summit of Ben Shian. At 1800 feet (549 metres) it gives extensive views of the surrounding countryside but it is only for the active.

**Hill Walks**   There are innumerable long-distance hill walks in the area over ancient paths. I have listed them below, but do remember that they are for the properly equipped, experienced walker.

*Balquhidder to Glen Dochart*—five and a half miles—1800 feet (549 metres) altitude.
*Loch Lubnaig to Loch Earn*—seven miles by Glen Ample—1050 feet (320 metres) altitude.
*Balquidder to Brig o' Turk*—eleven miles—1330 feet (405 metres) of climbing.
*Callander to Ardvorlich (Loch Earn).* Twelve miles by Meall na h Iolaire—1900 feet (579 metres) elevation; fourteen miles by Allt an Dubh Choirein—1800 feet (549 metres) elevation. The former though shorter has more climbing.
*Callander to Comrie by Glen Artney*—sixteen to seventeen miles—1000 feet (305 metres) elevation. This walk continues from a shorter forest walk to Bracklinn Falls and starts in the main car park in Callander.
In addition there are enough high hills to satisfy the most enthusiastic climber—Ben Vorlich 3224 feet (983 metres); Ben Ledi 2873 feet (876 metres); Ben Vane 2685 feet (818 metres); Ben More 3843 feet (1174 metres); Stob Binnein 3821 feet (1165 metres); The Tarmachans, all over 3000 feet (914 metres), are within striking distance of Strathyre.

**Strathyre Cabins**   At the south end of Loch Lubnaig there are seventeen fully-furnished log cabins, available for rent all year. Charges vary from £45 to £160 a week (for season 1981-82). For full particulars write to Forestry Commission Headquarters. These cabins are all of the one type and sleep five adults. Cots are available. These cabins were the first of their kind and were designed and erected by local labour.

Callander, a large busy tourist centre where all your shopping needs can be met is four miles away. Stirling is about threequarters of an hour away by car. There is a safari park at Blair Drummond and a collection of vintage cars at Doune. Boating is available on Loch Lubnaig, as is fishing. Pony Trekking is available at a local stables. This is an area full of interest and I have therefore included a map of the area showing all the major facilities.

# The Trossachs

This area is famous for the beauty of its scenery. It was the homeland of outlaw Rob Roy McGregor, celebrated in Scott's novel *Rob Roy*, and was the setting of Scott's poem "Lady of the Lake." During the last century Glasgow Corporation acquired Loch Katrine and the surrounding catchment area as a reservoir to supply the city's drinking water. The corporation runs a steamer, appropriately called *Sir Walter Scott* on the loch. The area, only forty miles away from Glasgow, has always been an attraction to its residents.

The Forestry Commission declared the whole area a Forest Park in 1953 in commemoration of the present Queen's coronation, and called it the "Queen Elizabeth Forest Park." It includes the forests of Achray, Loch Ard, and Buchanan, covers 17,000 hectares of land and stretches from Callander to Loch Lomond. There is a spread of facilities throughout the park but the major concentration can be found on the A821 known as the Duke's Pass.

**David Marshall Lodge**

This visitor centre is an impressive building on a hill to the north of Aberfoyle. It is a spectacular setting with fine, extensive views over the Carse of Forth. There is a large car park round a pleasant lochan with just enough birch trees to give a forest feeling. The grass is kept short enough to give everyone a bit of grass to picnic on. The lodge is open from 11.00 to 19.00 every day from mid March to mid October. The lodge has a large south facing terrace with a recently opened display area showing forestry, forest recreation, local history, and wildlife displays. During the summer a cafeteria is open.

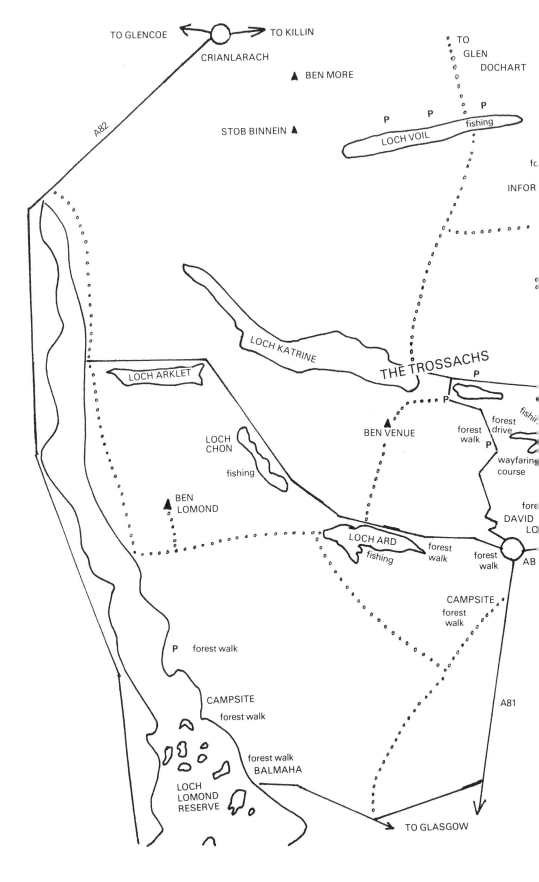

TO GLENCOE ← CRIANLARACH → TO KILLIN

TO GLEN DOCHART

A82

▲ BEN MORE

STOB BINNEIN ▲

P    P    P
LOCH VOIL    fishing

fo

INFOR

LOCH KATRINE

THE TROSSACHS    P

LOCH ARKLET

P

P

BEN VENUE ▲    forest walk    forest drive    fishi

LOCH CHON

P

fishing    wayfaring course

BEN LOMOND ▲

fore
DAVID
LO

LOCH ARD    forest walk

fishing    forest walk

AB

CAMPSITE
forest walk

P    forest walk

A81

CAMPSITE
forest walk

forest walk
BALMAHA

LOCH LOMOND RESERVE

TO GLASGOW

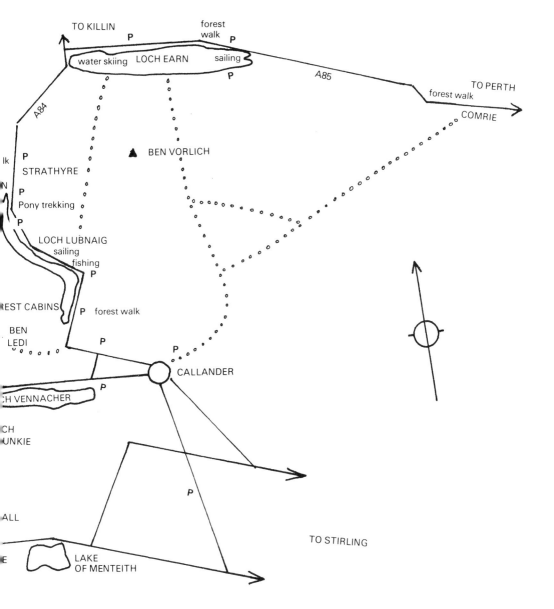

TO KILLIN

P    forest walk    P

water skiing    LOCH EARN    sailing

P

A85    TO PERTH

forest walk

A84    COMRIE

lk

P

STRATHYRE    ▲ BEN VORLICH

P

Pony trekking

P

LOCH LUBNAIG

sailing

fishing

P

REST CABINS    P    forest walk

BEN LEDI    P    P    CALLANDER

CH VENNACHER    P

CH UNKIE

P

TO STIRLING

ALL

E    LAKE OF MENTEITH

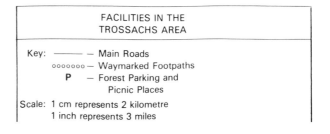

| FACILITIES IN THE TROSSACHS AREA |
|---|

Key: ——— — Main Roads
ooooooo — Waymarked Footpaths
P — Forest Parking and Picnic Places

Scale: 1 cm represents 2 kilometre
1 inch represents 3 miles

An information counter is manned and a large range of Forestry Commission publications is available. A short interpretative trail leads off to a waterfall on the burn below the lodge and there are numerous informal walks through the woods.

**Achray Forest Drive**

On the right two and a half miles north of Aberfoyle on the Duke's Pass can be found this forest drive where for £1 (1980) you can drive for seven miles through the forest. There are plenty of picnic areas and a children's play area beside the major car park. Toilets can be found there and several waymarked walks:

*A family enjoy a picnic by the lochside on the Achray Forest Drive, Queen Elizabeth Park.*

*Hilltop Viewpoint*, three miles north of Aberfoyle is a short walk (quarter mile) to an indicator board.
*Achray Forest Wayfaring Course.* Packs for the course are available from David Marshall Lodge. The course starts one mile northwards from the lodge on the Duke's Pass (see Glentress Wayfaring course for more details).

*Wildering Forest Circular Walks.* These start from Leanach car park about three and a half miles from Aberfoyle on the Duke's Pass. The total distance is up to five miles. Select your walk on display map at car park. *Gleann Riabhach Bronse Ring Walk.* This starts from rear of Achray Hotel, five and a half miles north of Aberfoyle and is two miles long.

**Fishing**

Fishing is available on three lochs, all accessible from Duke's Pass; Lochs Drunkie, Achray, and Reoidhte. Drunkie and Achray have brown trout and Pike while Reoidhte is stocked with rainbows and brown trout. All are bank fishing only. Vehicular access can be had by purchasing a Forest Drive ticket. Permits are available from Forestry Commission, Achray Forest Office, Aberfoyle, *Tel* 08772 383.

# Loch Ard Forest

This extensive forest spreads out to the south of Loch Ard and has in addition to a campsite many miles of pleasant forest walks just thirty miles from Glasgow.

**Cobleland Campsite**

This class A campsite is situated on the banks of the River Forth with plenty of trees round about for shelter. It can be found two miles south of Aberfoyle just off the A81 on the unclassified road to Gartmore. It is open from 1 April to 1 October and has 140 pitches. Unfortunately it has no facilities for the disabled and no advance booking facility.

There are waymarked walks from the campsite, but at the time of writing these were being replanned, so I would advise you to enquire of the camp warden who will be pleased to direct you.

Loch Ard is a large uniform plantation on rolling terrain with few outstanding features, for a stranger that is, so I recommend that unless you are an excellent navigator you stick to the waymarked routes.

*Doon Fairy Hill Trail.* This starts from a small car park at Balleich up the Manse Road in Aberfoyle and leads to a "Fairy Knowe." The trail is one mile in length.

*Loch and Lochan Walk*. The walk is three and a half miles, and starts from a small car park at Milton, one mile west of Aberfoyle on the B829 Kinlochard road.
*Loch Ard Forest Silver Ring Walk*. This walk is six miles and starts from Aberfoyle car park in the Manse Road.
*Highland Edge Walk*. This starts from Braeval car park, one mile east of Aberfoyle on the A81 road to Stirling and Callander. To complete the circuit of five miles involves some steepish climbing but the route to the viewpoint is fairly easy and can be retraced. For the long distance walker the path continues along the face of the Menteith Hills to the east of Loch Vennacher and then to Callander. The escarpment of the Menteith Hills is quite spectacular and can be imagined as the start of the Highlands. In fact they are part of the Old Red Sandstone belt which flanks the Central Valley Carboniferous layers. The actual fault lies behind them. I always think of them as the Highland edge and begin to sense the freedom that the mountains bring. The walk from Aberfoyle to Callander is about eight miles and you should try to arrange for a car to bring you back.

**Ben Venue**
The climb up Ben Venue (NN475064) at 2393 feet (729 metres) is worth it for the view, and for the sense of achievement in climbing a rugged little mountain. The route is waymarked by blue chevrons on the north approach and green ones on the southern route. The northern route starts at Achray Hotel while the southern one starts on Loch Ard at Ledard Burn near the Forest Hills Hotel, four and a half miles west of Aberfoyle on the B829. The waymarkers meet at a col at about 2000 feet (610 metres), the route to the summit being a further quarter mile to the north west. You should be properly equipped for this climb with map, compass, boots, waterproofs, spare clothing, extra food, and should have left details of your route and your estimated time of arrival back at your car.

The Forestry Commission has a free leaflet on the walks in the Forest Park and also has a map indicating most walks. The map is diagrammatic and must be used in conjunction with 1/50000 O.S. Sheets Nos. 56 and 57.

**Kinlochard to Rowardennan**
This long-distance route winds up the Bruach Coaruinn Burn to the Halfway Well, 1700 feet (518 metres) high

on the shoulder of Ben Lomond, then descends to Rowardennan. The routes and details of the colour-coded waymarkers are posted at the main forest access points. Apparently coloured discs (much used in the West Conservancy) are being replaced by the standard green post with coloured rings and arrows incised in the top six inches. The code works by each destination being given a colour. For example, no matter which routes you are on if you are heading for Kinlochard you should be following the blue chevrons (discs). Details are listed below:

Aberfoyle — yellow
Kinlochard — blue
Trossachs — green (Brig o' Turk)
Callander — black
Gartmore — orange (Cobleland Campsite)
Old Drymen/Gartmore Road — brown
Rowardennan — red
Inversnaid — white

The system has been in operation for about twenty years; I can remember coming across coloured discs when, as a boy, I was setting foot on the high tops for the first time. The value of waymarkers is that in a very popular area some form of guidance and control is considered necessary when half the walkers will be inexperienced.

**Fishing**

Loch Chon, eight miles west of Aberfoyle on the B829. Trout fishing with boats available. Permits from: Mr C. MacNair, Frenich Farm, Aberfoyle, Tel 087786 243.

# Loch Lomondside

The east side of Loch Lomond is probably the busiest forest area in Scotland. One hour from Glasgow, it is unrivalled for the variety of scenery it offers, and includes Ben Lomond, the most southerly Munro (the name given to peaks over 3000 feet (914 metres) of the Highlands). I am sure part of the attraction of that mountain is that it is visible from most parts of the city.

Most of the city's mountaineers cut their first boots, if not teeth, on its flanks. I certainly did. I remember once cycling the thirty odd miles to Rowardennan, climbing the Ben, and cycling back on the same day. I was definitely fitter then.

Most of the facilities lie within Buchanan Forest and start at the busy village of Balmaha, so I will start there too.

**Balmaha Walks**  Start in the local authority car park at Balmaha. One walk is called Gentle while the other is named Steep. Both are one and a half miles long. The gentle walk is mainly through plantations while the Steep climbs to two separate viewpoints.

**Loch Lomond National Nature Reserve**  The Reserve involves five islands on Loch Lomond and is managed by the Nature Conservancy. They have a nature trail on Inchcailloch which can be reached by boat from Balmaha. These islands and parts of surrounding hillsides are clothed in semi-natural Oak/mixed broadleaved woodland most of which was planted during the eighteenth century and managed on a coppice system to provide charcoal for iron smelting and bark for tannin extraction.

To contact the Nature Conservancy Council telephone 03606 428, or enjoy a walk through beautiful policies—Balloch Park to Balloch Castle, the Council's Regional Offices.

**Blair Picnic Place**  This picnic spot can be found two miles north of Balmaha on the road to Rowardennan. Because of the impracticality of collecting litter from such a busy area the Forestry Commission has designated the whole east Lochside a *Litter Free Area*. There are no litter bins so you must take away your rubbish. It appears to be working and is a concept which could perhaps be adopted elsewhere. There is a short lochside walk from the car park.

**Cashel Campsite**  A well-wooded site two and a half miles from Balmaha with 200 pitches and the usual shops and toilets befitting a class A site. There are also toilets for the disabled. The site is open from 1 April to 1 October, and for a stay of

94

seven nights or more there are advance booking facilities for a small fee and fourteen days' notice. The site has a lochside frontage so there is ample opportunity for boating, but I would advise you to have insect repellant available during the summer months.

**Sallochy Car Park and Trails**

A pleasant wooded car park with a shingle beach and barbecue which can be hired by parties (contact the Forester at *Tel* Drymen 255). The trail starts at the car park and is mainly concerned with the interpretation of the vegetation, wildlife, iron smelting, and old farming townships. The booklet is well written by Dr Roger Tippet of Glasgow University and is essential for a full appreciation of the trail. It is available from the forest office, camp shop, or local information office.

**Rowardennan Car Park**

A large very busy car park at the end of the road where there are toilets, an excellent notice board, full of information, beach, pier, hotel, youth hostel, and the starting point for two popular walking routes.

**Ben Lomond**

Ben Lomond is 3192 feet (973 metres). The path to the top starts from Rowardennan car park. It is a relatively easy climb for the fit but remember the top half of the mountain is very dangerous and has claimed a few lives, not least one noted climber. It is very popular so the path is well worn and muddy in places. You may be lucky and see some of the Ben's wild goat population.

**Rowardennan to Inversnaid**

This has always been a popular walk and the Commission has it waymarked with white markers. It follows a forest road for most of its length and is now part of the Highland Way, a long-distance walk from Glasgow to Fort William. It was commissioned by the Countryside Commission for Scotland and has an official guide of its own plus its own distinctive markers. From Rowardennan to Ardlui is its wildest stretch as it mostly follows old roads and paths. Contact: The Countryside Commission, Battleby House, Redgorton, Perth, *Tel* 0738 27921.

And so we move westwards into my next area, the Western Highlands.

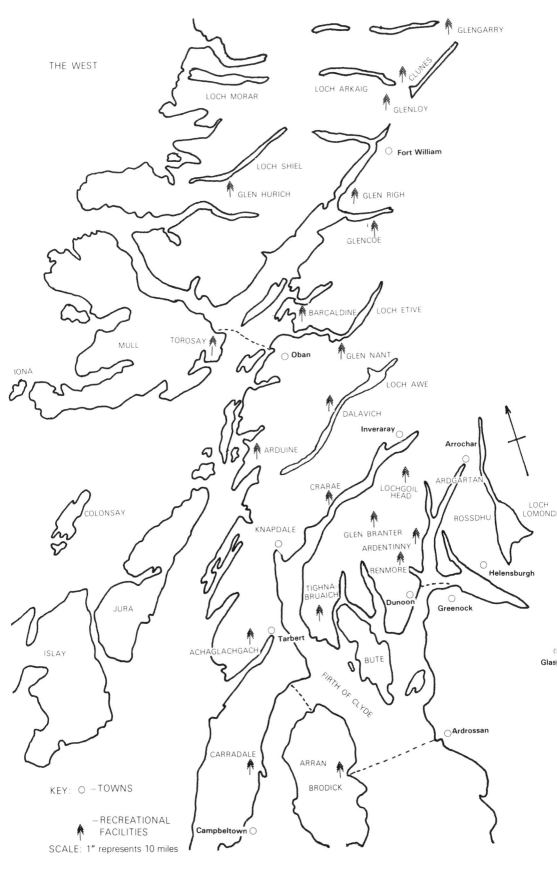

THE WEST

GLENGARRY

CLUNES

LOCH MORAR

LOCH ARKAIG

GLENLOY

○ **Fort William**

LOCH SHIEL

GLEN HURICH

GLEN RIGH

GLENCOE

MULL

TOROSAY

BARCALDINE

LOCH ETIVE

IONA

○ **Oban**

GLEN NANT

LOCH AWE

DALAVICH

**Inveraray** ○

**Arrochar**

ARDUINE

ARDGARTAN

COLONSAY

CRARAE

LOCHGOIL HEAD

ROSSDHU

LOCH LOMOND

KNAPDALE

GLEN BRANTER

ARDENTINNY

○ **Helensburgh**

BENMORE

JURA

TIGHNA-BRUAICH

**Dunoon** ○

**Greenock** ○

ISLAY

ACHAGLACHGACH

**Tarbert** ○

BUTE

FIRTH OF CLYDE

Glas

CARRADALE

ARRON

**Ardrossan** ○

BRODICK

KEY: ○ –TOWNS

– RECREATIONAL FACILITIES

SCALE: 1″ represents 10 miles

**Campbeltown** ○

# The West

The boundaries of this area are the Firth of Clyde in the south; Loch Lomond, Glen Falloch with its A82 road, and a line through the high wilds of the Grampian Mountains to Loch Laggan in upper Glen Spean on the A86 in the east; and then westwards through Glen Garry to Loch Hourn and the south tip of Skye. The western boundary is, of course, the Atlantic and its fringe of islands.

A huge geographical area this, with a coastline whose convolutions make it longer than that of Europe, the whole area has some spectacular scenery, from Arran, through hundreds of sea lochs, to the heights of Ben Nevis. The geology is very complex with coal deposits near Campbeltown, through Dalriadan shales and greywackes to the basalts of Mull and Morven, to the intrusive granites of Glen Etive, Rannoch Moor and Ben Nevis. The topography is often mountainous, but the whole area includes low-lying farmland in Kintyre as well as some of Scotland's highest hills — mountains which rise straight from the sea to well over 3000 feet (900 metres). The forest scenery is almost wholly coniferous, with a large number of older Forestry Commission Plantations and a great many young trees planted mainly by the Forestry Commission and the Forestry Management Companies. There were relatively few planting lairds in this part of the country, with a few notable exceptions such as the Duke of Argyll, so there are not many large older private plantations.

We finished the last section on the eastern banks of Loch Lomondside so we start this one on the bonnie western banks.

# Rossdhu House

On the A82 about seven miles north of Dumbarton, stands Rossdhu House, the home of Sir Ivor Colquhoun. The house has pleasant policies and attractive stands of semi-natural oak clothing the lower slopes of the loch, and house and grounds are usually open during the summer. When the long-awaited new road alignment takes place, the intention is to have picnic sites on the old road. A much-needed bonus for weary travellers on a busy road.

# Ardgartan Forest

Take the A83 at Tarbet to this steep forest on the shores of Loch Long. It is part of the Argyll Forest Park which was the first of its kind in Britain, and preceded the English National Parks concept by ten years. It was created in 1935 and embraces 26,000 hectares in the forests of Ardgartan, Glenbranter and Benmore. All three forests contain older plantations so the combinations of fine stands of spruce, sea lochs and rugged moutains make this an area of outstanding beauty.

**Ardgartan Campsite**
This class A campsite on the promontory of the River Coe nestles beneath Ben Arthur (nicknamed "The Cobbler" because of the shape of its summit crags). It is two miles west of Arrochar on the A83, and a very busy site being just over an hour from Glasgow. Open from 14 March to 28 October it accepts advance bookings for seven days or more for a fee and on fourteen days' notice. Unfortunately there are no facilities for the disabled.

The site has loch frontage so boat-launching is easy and sea fishing on Loch Long is worthwhile with large cod and skate being available for the skilful angler.

Contact: Forestry Commission, Ardgartan Campsite, Arrochar, Dunbartonshire, *Tel* Arrochar 293. For members of the Camping Club of Great Britain, there is a small campsite south of the Commission site.

The waymarked walks are all long-distance hill walks although plenty of short walks can be found on the forest roads. The walks are colour coded and remember that you might find some coloured discs instead of the standard coloured incised rings.

*Blue Walk*, Ardgartan to Lochgoilhead via Corlessan Glen. Six miles, 1550 feet (472 metres) elevation. Starts at the Forest Office.
*Yellow Walk*, Ardgartan to Lochgoilhead via the peninsula known as "Argyll's Bowling Green." Twelve miles. No great elevation but a lot of forest road walking. Starts at Forest Office.
*Green Walk*, Carrick Castle to Ardentinny. Five miles. Pretty rough. Starts at end of unclassified road five miles south of Lochgoilhead.
*Red Walk*, Lettermay to Strachur via Curra Lochan. Eight miles. Hill walk. 1100 feet (335 metres) elevation. Starts one mile south west of Lochgoilhead on unclassified road.
*Orange Walk*, Lettermay to Strachur via Lochain nan Cnaimh. Eight miles. 1800 feet (549 metres) elevation. Rough going.
*Red Walk*, Circular three-mile walk from Lochgoilhead round Donich Glen.

Relevant 1/50,000 O.S. sheet No. 56.

Remember you are in a high rainfall area and rough high hills so observe the mountain code. For a more detailed description of the many walks available and very full information about the Forest Park I suggest you buy the Guide to Argyll Forest Park from the camp shop. There are two stopping points—a spectacular one at the top of the Rest and Be Thankful and one beside a mountain stream in Gleann Mor. There is a small arboretum in Lochgilphead for an evening stroll.

There is bank fishing for salmon and sea trout for a limited number of rods on the east bank of the River Goil. Contact, The Forestry Commission, Forest Office, Ardgartan, Arrochar, *Tel* Arrochar 243.

| **Climbing** | Some good climbing in "The Arrochar Alps" is available for the experienced. |
| --- | --- |

We will stay in the Forest Park and move down into Cowal on the A815 road to Dunoon. (Another, more restful, approach from the south is to cross on the ferry from Gourock direct to Dunoon). As you travel eastwards along Loch Eck through Glenbranter Forest there are two pleasant picnic stops by the side of Loch Eck.

# Benmore Forest

Finart Bay Picnic Place at Ardentinny provides a pleasant stop with a shingle beach, toilets and the start of the walk to Carrick Castle.

| **Fishing** | River Finart — sea trout. Contact: The Forestry Commission, Benmore, Kilmun, *Tel* Kilmun 308. |
| --- | --- |
| **Kilmun** | Kilmun Arboretum: Forestry Commission research plantations with a wide variety of trees, especially Eucalyptus. The guide book is essential and is available from Forestry Commission office. |
| **Younger Botanic Gardens** | The Younger Botanic Gardens is a must. An annexe of the Royal Botanic Gardens these gardens have a beautiful collection of rhododendrons and a breathtaking avenue of sequoias or Coast Redwoods. The booklet, too, is an attractive souvenir of your holiday. The best time to visit will be in May. For additional information about the many walks in Cowal, both waymarked and unmarked, the local tourist association has an excellent series of maps and leaflets. |

Our route now continues on the A836 to the A8003 on the road to Tighnabruaich and Glendaruel Forest.

An excellent viewpoint is available on the new A8003 where it passes through the plantation at the Jubilee Picnic Place. Not far from there is *Caladh Castle* Forest Trail, which is only for the fit as it descends steeply to the lochside.

Tighnabruaich has always been a popular holiday spot (despite the midges in late summer) and there are a number of picnic places and walks. A booklet is available from Forestry Commission offices throughout the area. There are also Wildlife Observation Hides available. Contact: The Forestry Commission, Glendaruel Forest, Hafton, Tighnabruaich. *Tel* Tighnabruaich (0700 81) 284.

The last time I was there I saw a golden eagle; I am told that it nests thereabouts, so you stand a chance of spotting our biggest bird.

Drive on round on the B8000 for a scenic drive but remember to take care as you will be driving on a single track road. It brings you back to the A83 where the next place of forestry interest is Cairndow House which reputedly now has Britain's tallest tree. Carry on to Inverary Castle, home of the Duke of Argyll, with its fine policies and plantations. South of here at Minard (still on the A83) is Crarae Gardens with many fine and unusual specimens. All these houses and grounds are open to the public during the summer.

# Knapdale Forest

A beautiful forest planted between the wars has a variety of walks available from a walk round a pretty loch for all the family to a strenuous walk along a ridge above the Sound of Jura. The day my daughter and I chose gave a wonderful walk on a beautiful day, sustained by a plentiful supply of blaeberries. The forest boasts an Archaeological Walk for those interested. The forest stands in an area which was well populated, and there are numerous deserted shielings and crofting townships as well as some spectacular hill forts. A comprehensive booklet is available from the Forest Office or local Tourist Centre.

**Holiday House**   One fully furnished house is available in the forest village of Achnamara on an unclassified road four and a half miles south of the junction with the B8052 road to Tayvallich. It sleeps five with a cost range of £30-£105 (1981). It is usually fully booked so you will have to plan well ahead.

**Fishing**   Five lochs available:

| | | | |
|---|---|---|---|
| *Loch Coille Bhar* | NR 900 780 | Brown Trout | Two boats |
| *Loch Barnluasgan* | NR 910 790 | Brown Trout | One boat |
| *Loch Linnhe* | NR 900 790 | Brown Trout | One boat |
| *Loch Losgurn* | NR 891 790 | Brown Trout | Bank only |
| *Loch Seafield* | NR 888 788 | Brown Trout | Bank only |

(marked on O.S. maps as Lochan Buic)

Contact: Forestry Commission, Cairnbaan, Lochgilphead, *Tel* Lochgilphead 2304.

An outstanding feature of this forest and others in the west is the quantity (though sadly no quality) of broadleaved woods, and in particular, oakwoods. These are to be retained as refuges for wildlife, and to preserve their unique habitat for many plants and animal communities. Two interesting inhabitants of this forest are sika deer which have naturalised themselves after escaping from an estate further south in Kintyre. They were originally introduced from Japan. Many species of wood ants live in the exotic conifers which have built huge formicaria of dead needles, Look, but please do not disturb. In winter the many lochs are a haven for numerous water birds.

Worthy for inclusion if just for its name is Achaglachgach Forest, where fishing on Carse Burn is available. Contact: The Forestry Commission, Torinturk, Tarbert, *Tel* Tarbert 566.

# Carradale Forest

Carradale, on the east side of Kintyre, is a holiday village and the local forest has responded by having a small information centre, some pleasant forest walks and two picnic places. On a calm day Grogport can be recommended. It is on the shore, five miles north of Carradale on the B842. There are fine views over the Kilbrandon Sound to Arran and it is a good place for a family holiday or full-day trip.

This is a convenient point to cross the Sound to the Clyde Islands of Arran and Bute. A ferry operates between Lochranza and Claonaig during the summer but it is small so try and book ahead. Both, of course, are very popular holiday resorts with a full range of facilities. That is where the similarity ends. Bute is a lowland island with rich agricultural land. It has some mixed woodland belonging to the Marquis of Bute. There are some pleasant woodland walks in Skipper and Skeoch Woods near Rothesay and at Loch Fad. A guide book is available from the Tourist Office on the pier.

Arran, as well as being bigger, is in the northern half very much a "Highland" island with some very fine mountains. The highest—Goat Fell at 2866 feet (874 metres)—is a National Trust property as are the beautiful gardens around Brodick Castle. The Forestry Commission has a 6000 hectare forest of young trees and has constructed two picnic sites. One is off the A841, two miles south of Brodick, and the other off the "Ross Road" half a mile from Lamlash Bay.

There are plenty of walks, both marked and unmarked, and a visit to the forest or information office will provide you with all the necessary information. Remember, you will be walking among steep-sided mountains so wear good boots.

The main approach to Arran is by ferry from Ardrossan while the ferry to Bute is from Wemyss Bay. Both are on the Ayrshire coast but both islands have links with Argyll—at Colintraive for Bute and Claonaig for Arran.

Our next step is Inverliever Forest where the Forestry Commission has a major recreational development.

# Inverliever Forest

This is a large forest of 9000 hectares, the management of which was acquired from the Crown Commissoners on the Forestry Commission's inception in 1919. From these beginnings the forest has grown to its present size by planting and merging with two other forests – Inverinan and part of Raera. Some of the early plantings are still there, and it is worth a visit to the magnificent trees in McKenzie's Grove to see the big Sitka Spruce. The forest is found on the west side of Loch Awe and centres on the forest village of Dalavich (NM 986 126) on the unclassified road which runs from Ford (B840) to Kilchrenan (B845). Your route can be from the A816 just north of Kilmartin to Ford, or from the A85 at Taynuilt to Kilchrenan.

**Loch Aweside Forest Cabins** This new development opened in May this year and consists of forty-four log cabins of varying designs. All sleep six people and are available fully furnished all of the year. The cost range in 1981 is £55-£160 per week with electricity and VAT extra. A cot is available if required and a few cabins have been specially modified for the disabled. The cabins are very appealing and I know our three-year-old adored her holiday in one – she still talks about it.

The cabins have been specially built so that each has a view of the loch and are a northern extension of Dalavich village. There is a new community centre, in the same architectural style, available for both visitors and residents. You can enjoy a drink and compare adventures, play billiards, darts, table tennis, badminton or carpet bowls. Loch Awe, as well as being nice to look at, is also good to fish in and boats, both rowing and powered, are available for hire. Contact the site manager or forest office. Fishing is also available in Loch Avich, about six miles away on the Kilmelford road, where there is a boat as well as bank fishing by fly only for brown trout. The rivers *Avich* and *Liever* are available for salmon and sea trout which run late in the season, depending on the weather. In addition there are hill lochs which will involve a fair amount of walking;

but what could be nicer than a walk to a lonely hill loch, a few hours' fishing, then back to the cabin through the gloaming with tomorrow's breakfast in your basket?

The lochs are:

*A view of the timber-built cabins at Lochaweside, Inverliever Forest.*

*Loch Nant*, NN 200 240. A four- or five-mile walk to this Hydro-Electric reservoir. Brown trout. Permits from Kilchrenan Trading Post.

*Loch Tromlee*, MN 040 250. Bank fishing for Pike. Permits from Kilchrenan Trading Post.

*The Cam, Eun Lochs, Lochan Dubh* and other hill lochs. Brown trout. All involve a lot of walking. Permits from Ford Post Office.

Facilities for youth organisation camping exist. Contact: Forestry Commission, Portcullis House, India Street, Glasgow.

**Youth Campsite**

There are, in addition, plenty of waymarked walks and picnic places up and down the length of Loch Awe. Some of the viewpoints are spectacular, as the road climbs to about 190 metres above the loch. The walks, while involving some beautiful and interesting features such as Avich Falls, could be better routed and, no doubt, this will in time be done. One thing I did like was the siting of picnic tables on the Avich Falls walk, but some notification in the booklet would have encouraged me to carry our lunch there instead of just wishing that I had!

The whole area is relatively quiet and, with a considerable area of oakwoods within the forest area, good opportunities to watch wildlife exist. Remember that you will have to be up at dawn (or preferably before as you should be in position as dawn breaks) to do any worthwhile animal watching. The whole area is very attractive and scenically beautiful and well worth considering as a base for a Highland Forest Holiday.

Two nearby places to visit are over to the west on the main coast road from Lochgilphead to Oban (A816).

**Arduaine** This is a lovely sheltered garden beside Loch Melford Hotel which is especially good in late May, early June when the rhododendrons are in blossom. (NM 790 100).

**Lunga Wildlife Reserve** This is further south on the same road; it has featured on television, as wolves were once kept by the owner. (NM 811 083).

Both Arduaine and Lunga can be reached by driving over the hill road from Loch Aweside past Loch Avich to Kilmelford on a spectacular single track road with superb views and many hairpin bends and taxing gradients.

**Glen Nant National Nature Reserve** This is an important woodland reserve jointly run by the Nature Conservancy Council and the Forestry Commission. It can be found on the B845 Taynuilt to Kilchrenan road, one mile south of Taynuilt. It is the single largest remnant of the Ancient Forest of Lorn, comprising oak, ash, hazel and alder complexes. There is a Nature Trail on Forestry Commission land, two and a half miles long, with interpretative panels.

# Barcaldine Forest

This forest is on the A828 Oban to Fort William road. You cross Connel Bridge over the Falls of Lora, which are tidal rapids at the mouth of Loch Etive, and travel northwards.

## Ben Lora Walk

Created for the busy caravan parks round Benderloch, this has a car park at Benderloch and two steep walks to viewpoints over the Firth of Lorne to Mull.
Lower Walk: (Red markers) one mile.
Summit Walk: (Blue markers) two and threequarter miles to the top of Ben Lora, 1010 feet (308 metres).

On the way north, one mile south of Barcaldine, Saint Columba's Bay picnic site has been laid out on the line of the old road. Every parking bay has a sea view.

## Glen Dubh

Two miles further on just past Barcaldine village is the car park for these fine walks. Take care or you might miss it as there is no advance warning sign — surely an essential on a fast main road. The car park is in a stand of old Douglas fir, called Sutherland's Grove, which are 110 years old, and well worth a visit. There are three walks, designed on a standard lay-out: *Short Walk (yellow)*, threequarters of a mile, *Middle Walk (red)*, one and a quarter miles, *Long Walk (blue)*, one and threequarter miles.

There is a spectacular start up a river gorge and over a narrow bridge, which children will love or hate.

## Eas Na Circe

There is a car park on a picnic site near the head of Loch Creran, and a walk of two and a quarter miles through youngish plantations, past Eas na Circe (Torrent of the Grouse) to a forest road.

## Fishing

*Glen Dubh Reservoir:* (NM 976 423), brown trout, boat available.
*Loch Dubh Mor:* (NB 948 389), bank fishing only for brown trout.

Contact the Forestry Commission, Forest Office, Barcaldine, Connel, *Tel* 063172 203.

# Glen Coe Forest

Perhaps one of the most famous tourist glens in Scotland because of the notorious "Massacre of Glen Coe." The Forestry Commission has responded to public pressure and provided the following recreational facilities:

**Glen Coe Campsite** A Class A site with 200 pitches, open from 1 April to 1 October. There is also a limited service during the winter for the winter climbing and skiing enthusiast. The site is on the A82, one mile east of Glencoe village. There are toilet facilities for the disabled. The rugged parts of Glen Coe—Aonach Eagach, Bidean nan Bian and their outliers—all belong to the National Trust, and no development is permitted to take place within its boundaries. The climber or skiier will really need a car to cover the whole range of mountains.

**Signal Rock Trail** A one and a half mile walk through plantations to Signal Rock, used by the MacDonald chiefs to summon their clansmen. The walk can start at three possible places, although I suggest you use the National Trust Information Centre car park on the A82 and combine a walk with a visit to the Centre, where there are good displays about the Glen, an information desk, a ranger service, coffee shop, toilets and a good supply of maps and literature for sale. Buy a booklet in the Centre.

**Lochan Trail** On the unclassified road through Glencoe village or Carnoch, at the east end of the street, a side road goes up to the hospital and a car park for a two-mile walk round an artificial lochan to a viewpoint. During the summer make a point of finding the lily pond as there are some very pretty lilies growing there. It would be possible to push a wheelchair round the loch if the pusher is fit!

**Fishing** Bank fishing in this stocked lochan for brown trout and rainbow trout. Permits from the Camp Shop or Forest Office. Glenahulish, Ballachulish, *Tel* 08552 268.

There are plenty walks and climbs in Glen Coe. Most are only for the experienced walker or climber, although the Highland Way goes over the Devil's Staircase at the east end of the glen which has plenty of markers and is patrolled by a ranger, so that stage might be a good introduction to the hills if you are there in the summer. For the more ambitious there are plenty of good guide books available.

If on your way north you decide to go straight north on the A82, you will certainly pass some magnificent scenery in Glen Falloch, Strath Fillan, Loch Tulla and Rannoch Moor. Most forestry plantations in the region are very young but at these particular areas there are remnants of the old Caledonian Pine Forest. Remember that they are all privately owned, and it is best just to view them from the road as these woods have a tenuous hold on life and cannot stand much disturbance.

Our route to the north takes us over the splendid new bridge at Ballachulish, and you move into the North Conservancy and *Glen Righ Forest*. A road to the right marked Inchree takes you to a quiet picnic place with a short one-mile walk to a waterfall. A very useful large picnic place known as *Loch Linnhe Picnic Place* has been constructed between the main A82 and the loch, about eight miles from Ballachulish Bridge. The facility to launch small boats exists although I have never seen it done.

One mile from there is a car park called *Corriechurachan*. It is a little difficult to find; travelling northwards you must turn right across the traffic into a forest road. A steepish walk, mainly by forest road, takes you to a viewpoint over the loch and the hills of Morven behind.

The busy town of Fort William is surrounded by a forest known as *Leanachan* which has a quiet car park in the hills above the town at *Lundubhra*. Go right at the roundabout on the south side of the town and climb up past the new houses and over the hill for about four miles. There is a walk along Wade's Military Road which is now part of the West Highland Way.

Other walks are:

*Achbriabhach* Positioned at the top of Glen Nevis below Ben Nevis, there is a short waymarked walk along a forest road. Just for the sake of going up the Glen, I would suggest that you visit this walk. If you are properly booted, walk through the gorge at the head of the glen to Steall where you can see how tenaciously the birch cling to the rocky ledges. This is a good example of a hanging valley which has a flattish surface from glacial deposits. Turn right just before the distillery at the north end of the town.

*Glen Loy* On the B8005 off the A830 Mallaig Road at Banavie there are two walks through middle-aged plantations. This is where to come for the best views of Ben Nevis.

*Clunes* About five or six miles futher on there are three walks of varied forest. The car park at *Ciag* is worth a visit after rain just to see and hear the large waterfall. If you like driving to out of the way places, continue driving up the side of Loch Arkaig for fine views of indigenous Scots Pine Forest on the south side of the loch. These, and the older woods you have driven through, belong to Cameron of Locheil over whose land the British Commandos trained during World War II.

A map showing all these forest walks is available from information offices.

Our journey now takes us further westwards to the wilds of Moidart, Morven and Ardnamurchan, our most westerly mainland piece of land. Consult you map, as you have a choice of route: overland by A830 and B861 or across Corran Ferry on the A82 south of Fort William. We are making for *Sunart Forest* where, in conjunction with the Nature Conservancy Council, an Interpretative Nature Trail has been laid down in Strontian Glen Oakwoods. A waterfall, old lead mines and the typical oakwood ecosystem feature on this walk. The booklet is essential and is available at the local information centre. For more detailed information contact: Nature Conservancy Council at Inverness 39431, one and a half miles north of Strontian on the road to Glen Hurich, signposted *Arundle*. Three picnic sites have been constructed at Arundle in conjunction with the trail:

**Glenhurich**

NM 836 666. Possibly the most out of the way of our mainland forests worth visiting, if just to say you have been there. Good views of Loch Doilet and Loch Sheil.

**Ardery**

NM 745 620. A coastal picnic spot six miles west of Strontian with a walk along low cliffs on Loch Sunart.

**Camastorsa**

One mile beyond Salen on the A861. A lochside spot with boat launching.

Journey on to Lochaline (A884) through splendid scenery. (I keep repeating myself here but no matter where you go the scenery of mountain, sea and loch is magnificent.) A ferry crosses here to *Mull*, a large island which really demands a holiday in itself. The Forestry Commission has walks and car parks on the island:

**Aros**

Half a mile east of *Tobermory* on A848 is this small country park on the site of an old mansion with walks, toilets, play area, and a rhododendron collection.

**Ardmore**

In conjunction with Glengorm Estate, this fine cliff-top walk is to the most northerly point in the island. On the unclassified road to Glengorm Castle off the A8073 Tobermory to Dervaig road.

**Fishnish**

Just beside the ferry slip from Lochaline, a small picnic area has been constructed. Boat launching and paddling pool available.

**Fishing**

On Loch Frisa. Brown Trout. Permits from the Forest Office one mile north of Salen. *Tel* Aros 346.

**Torosay Castle**

Open to the public, and there are some interesting walks through the policies. Within walking distance of Craignure Pier.

We are now on our way to the north up the Great Glen from Fort William to Inverness on the A82. There are forest facilities in *Glen Garry Forest*, including a large, very useful, picnic place, two miles south-west of Invergarry overlooking Loch Oich. For a step off the beaten track, visit *Glengarry Picnic Place*. On a forest road off the A87 Invergarry to Kyle of Lochalsh road.

111

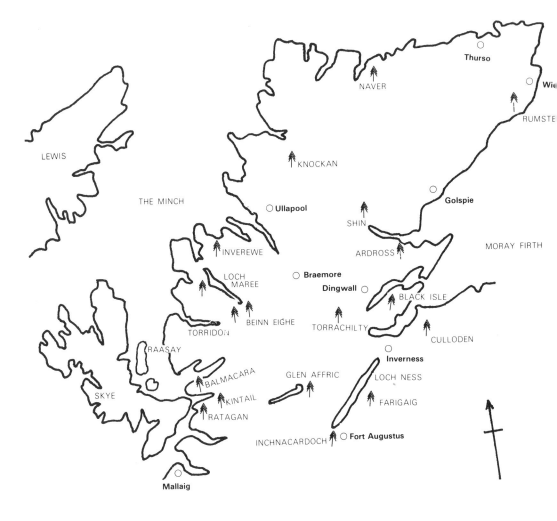

THE NORTH

KEY: —RECREATIONAL FACILITIES

O —TOWNS

SCALE: 1″ represents 20 miles approx.

# The Northern Highlands

My next area, from the Great Glen northwards, is another big one with broad expanses of mountain and moorland. Old mature spruce forests in Inchnacardoch, young Lodgepole pine forests of Sutherland, mature Scots pine forests in the Black Isle weave a matrix of green over large tracts of unbroken and, in many cases, uninhabited land with a long, indented coastline and a skerry of islands to the west. The rainfall gradient moves from around thirty inches a year in the east to over a hundred in the mountains of the west. The best way of enjoying a holiday in this part, if time is limited to a fortnight, would be to stay a week in the east, around Dornoch, and a week somewhere in the west. Remember that towns in the west are few and small and can become quickly crowded. Similarly, there are relatively few roads so traffic can be heavy and slow moving, especially towards important tourist centres like Ullapool.

## Inchnacardoch Forest

Inchnacardoch Forest centres on the town of Fort Augustus, and is one of the Forestry Commission's older forests. There is an interpretative trail—the booklet, packed with information, is essential for this—and there are two quiet picnic places beyond the forest office on the road to Auchterawe.

# Glen Urquhart Forest

Further up the Great Glen is *Glen Urquhart Forest*. Turn off the A82 in Lewiston for:

**Divach Falls Walk**  The falls are most impressive when the river is in spate. A pleasant walk through oakwoods.

**Reelig Glen Picnic Place and Walk**  Eight miles west of Inverness on the A9, take the left turn to *Moniack*. Two walks of one and a quarter and two and a half miles through old policy woodlands.

# Farigaig Forest

On the quiet east side of Loch Ness is *Farigaig Forest*. Here is a picnic area, information centre, two easy walks, two more difficult walks and toilets. This is a place to give a whole day to, as care has gone into the selection of the routes and the writing of the essential and informative booklet. There are good walks through broadleaved and coniferous forest, including some less usual conifers. Good views and waterfalls, although it can be steep in places.

The picnic area can be found on the B852 above Inverfarigaig. From Fort Augustus take the A862, then B852 to Foyers. About one mile from Foyers is the road to the right. There is another picnic place near Foyers — look out for the signs.

# Culloden Forest

The forest encompasses the busy town of Inverness. There is a walk at Craig Phadrig which is a vitrified fort just a mile out of town — a walk for a summer's evening when stopping in Inverness. Take the A9, turn left onto Leachkin Road at Muirtown basin; keep straight on, heading for Craig Dunain. The walk is short and steep, but worth it for the view.

On B9006 in conjunction with the National Trust, which has an information centre at the site of the battle, a trail through the pinewoods round the battle lines of the two opposing armies. Their clan and regimental stations are marked with posts. Except in heavy rain, ordinary footwear will do. Pushchairs possible — wheelchairs too difficult to complete the whole trail although short sections could be negotiated with difficulty.

**Culloden Moor Battlefield Trail**

A two-mile walk through mixed woodland. Booklet available from tourist office. Start near Smithton.

**Forest Trail**

# Affric Forest

Take the A831 off either the A9 or A82 to Cannich, then follow signs. Affric is a large forest, with one of our more important Caledonian Forest remnants. The scenery is classically and typically Highland. Do make sure you get a booklet as it is probably the best I came across with good, easily-read information, artistic and practical layout and a card to record your photographs.

Five miles from Cannich on the road to Affric Lodge are two walks. A shorter walk of one and a quarter miles through interesting pinewoods, with a longer circuit to a lochan of about two and a half miles. Toilets beside the car park.

**Dog Falls Walks**

Two short walks with viewpoints between Lochs Affric and Benevean.

**Affric River Walks**

Long-distance walks with many fine climbs abound in this area, but you should be very fit, experienced and equipped to bivouac. It is a good area for watching deer, but check at the forest office during August and September. Probably one of the finest cross-country

**Long Walks**

*Spectacular Loch Affric, Affric Forest.* routes is from Loch Duich via the Falls of Glomach. Only for the hardened walkers though.

**Fishing**  Loch Aigas, brown trout, boat available. Contact, The Forestry Commission, Cannich, *Tel* Cannich 272.

# Skye

Our road takes us over Mam Ratagan to the summer-only ferry to Skye at Glenelg. This is the route Dr Johnson and Boswell took to Skye. Skye is a large island and demands a holiday on its own. The Forestry Commission has a large forest area of over 21,000 hectares, and has constructed three car parks and laid out some walks. These are:

**Glen Brittle Car Park**  A tiered car park to provide everyone with a fine view of the Cuillins. Three miles off the B8009 road to Carbost.

**Glen Varrgill Picnic Site and Walks**

This lies half a mile south of Portree on A850. The walks are steep but fine views of Portree Bay are achieved by your exertion. Another fine evening walk if the midges allow it.

**Storr Car Park and Walk**

At the side of A855 seven miles north of Portree. A steep two-mile walk to the Old Man of Storr with superb views of islands, sea and mountains – my favourite combination of scenic elements. Picnic facilities at the car park. This walk can be very windy so make sure you come properly clad to keep the wind out and enjoy the walk.

**Raasay Walks**

For absolute peace, cross to Raasay and walk through the youngish plantations, mainly larch, that the Commission has on this off-shore island. Refresh your mind with quiet reflection.

**Kyle of Lochalsh**

Cross from Skye by way of Kyle of Lochalsh. Most of the peninsula belongs to the National Trust who have plenty of woodland walks round Lochalsh House at Balmacara, three and a half miles east of Kyle. They also have a countryside interpretative centre in the grounds which have, in common with most west coast policies, a good collection of rhododendrons and azaleas. A booklet is available which gives details of plenty of other walks throughout the property. Make sure you see the village of Plockton, beloved of photographers. There is a ranger service – contact *Tel* Balmacara 236 or 278.

# South Strome Forest

The Forestry Commission also has woodlands nearby in South Strome Forest. The facilities offered are:

**Balmacara Campsite**

The Class B campsite is found on a road to the north (left), half a mile on the Kyle side of Revaig village. A small, wooded site of only fifty pitches, and you *must* have your own toilet facilities. It is open from 1 May to 28 September and there are no advance booking facilities. Contact The Forestry Commission, South Strome Forest, Achmore, Stromeferry, Ross-shire, *Tel* Stromeferry 246.

**Strome Wood Walk** This pleasant walk of about one mile gives fine views of Loch Carron. It is located on a forest road near the junction of the A890 and the old Strome Ferry road. Picnicking facilities along the forest road.

**Loch Carron Viewpoint** A picnic site specially for motorists in a lay-by on the A890 close by the junction with the old ferry road. From this point you can travel up the coast on the A896 to Torridon. Take note of the old Caledonian Pinewood as you descend towards Shieldaig.

# Torridon

Property of National Trust for Scotland who have a visitor centre with deer museum at the junction of the A896 and Diabeg Road. There are Audio-visual displays, a guide book, ranger service, guided walks. Contact *Tel* Torridon 221.

Torridon with its sandstone and quartz mountains will always have a fond niche in my memory as I spent a magic fortnight's holiday when the sun shone all the time. I barnstormed all the available mountains with no effort. There were no midges that I can remember and the campsite company was convivial. What more could one ask for? The mountains are high, rugged and difficult so you should be properly equipped and experienced.

# Beinn Eighe

The farthest east of the Torridon hills, this was the first National Nature Reserve in Britain. It was acquired by the Nature Conservancy Council to protect and preserve the Caledonian Pinewoods thereabouts. There is a visitor centre at Aultroy Cottage on A832, north-west of Kinlochewe. Nature trails of great interest have been laid down through the pines. There are fine views northwards across Loch Maree to Slioch, a sugar loaf mountain. If you are especially lucky, you might catch a glimpse of our rarest forest animal—the pine marten. Contact, *Tel* Kinlochewe 254 and 244.

# Slattadale

Drive slowly down Loch Maree on the A832 savouring the views. Try to do it early one morning from east to west with the sun at your back. At *Slattadale* the Forestry Commission has a picnic site with two walks. Slattadale is on the A832 about twelve or thirteen miles west of Kinlochewe.

*Forest Walk*, a short one-mile circular walk through Norway Spruce. A booklet is available from information offices in the area.

*The Tollie Path*. This is a five-mile walk over an old path to Poolewe, with views back up Loch Maree so try to do it with the sun to your south-west. Boots or wellingtons will be essential, and a car to meet you desirable. Described in the booklet.

For motorists, a charming picnic site in open birchwood has been constructed on the south side of the A832 near Grudie Bridge Power Station.

# Inverewe Gardens

This National Trust property is not to be missed. It is a living testament to one man's determination to create a garden out of an exposed moorland. There is plenty of literature, both about the garden and its originator Osgood MacKenzie. The gardens are off the A832 just north of Poolewe. Information centre, restaurant. Contact, *Tel* Poolewe 229.

Half a mile from the junction of the A832 and the A835 main road to Ullapool is another National Trust property, *Corrieshalloch Gorge*, with a path to a view of the waterfall, and a steep-sided wooded gorge.

Four miles further on the Forestry Commission has a small arboretum at the plantation called *Lael*. There is a good car park with a steep two-mile walk through conifers and broadleaved trees. A booklet is available from Information centres. Steepness allows only the fit to complete the walk.

Loop round on the A835 through Ullapool to the

*Inverpolly National Nature Reserve* — a property, managed by the Nature Conservancy Council, of major geological importance.

**Knockan Visitor Centre** Thirteen miles north of Ullapool on the A835. Open May to mid-September. A guide book of the reserve and Nature Trail leaflet may be purchased here. Toilets. Guides available. There is a trail, one and a half miles. There are also, for the enthusiast, relics of relatively untouched primitive birch-hazel woodland. Contact, *Tel* Elphin 234 or Lochinver 204.

This is the turning point for our journey. For the more intrepid travellers who are going to the far north, the following forest recreational facilities are available:

# Naver Forest

**Borgie Walks** A short, sheltered walk in the north coast's only older plantation. The car park is on a forest road off the A836 just after Borgie Bridge.

**Rossal Trail** Interpretative trail round a pre-Clearance village. Found on a forest road just off the B873 at Syre.

**Rumster Forest Walk** An easy, pleasant walk through conifer plantations beside a stream; one and a half miles. Turn off the A9, half a mile south of Lybster onto the unclassified *Achavanich* road for two miles. Car park and picnic place.

# Shin Forest

Our next forest is *Shin Forest*, a large forest of 35,000 hectares, whose main area contains four walks, all of which have car parks with picnic facilities. A guide book is available from information centres. The walks are:

**Shin Falls Walk** One and a half miles long, this walk starts at Falls car park on the A836 Lairg to Bonar Bridge.

120

A walk of one and threequarter miles through sheltered larch woods. The start is on the A836 one mile north of Bonar Bridge.

**Drumliah Walk**

Two and a quarter miles through woodlands to a small loch. The start is just through the Castle gates on the Culrain road from Ardgay on the A9. Keep right at Culrain. There are fine views of Kyle of Sutherland.

**Carbisdale Castle Walks**

One and a half miles through a precipitous river gorge. Start on the forest road off Rosehall to Invershin road (A837), take first unclassified road to the left, then left again. The entry is a quarter of a mile left.

**Raven Rock Walk**

Eastwards to *Dornoch Forest* now and a car park with a picnic site and a one and a half mile walk along a burn; near Embo, three miles north of Dornoch. Another short, but steep, walk on the south side of the Kyle of Sutherland at *Morangie Forest Walk*, three to four miles west of Tain on the A9. Car parking, picnic place, a one-mile long walk through pine forests.

# Torrachilty Forest

Turn right off the A832 just after Contin. Turn right just before traffic lights on the bridge. The site is in a secluded situation beside the river. Toilets on site. The trail is three and a quarter miles through a variety of habitats, and a shorter walk is available. Guide book from forest office.

**Torrachilty Picnic Place and Trail**

A pleasant lochside site in open birchwoods. First left on A832 just after the traffic lights on the bridge north of Contin.

**Lochachilty Picnic Place**

From the Falls car park, two miles west of Contin on the A832, an attractive series of paths lead to the falls. Toilets at car park.

**Rogie Falls Walk**

Two miles west of Garve on the A835 Ullapool road. A riverside site among old pinewoods. Good scenery.

**Little Garve Picnic Place**

# The Black Isle

The last place on our journey is the Black Isle, across the firth from Inverness. Here the local tourist organisation has done commendable work and laid out and gathered the information for no less than nineteen different varied walks. The choice is enormous, from the Cromarty Coast walk to a forest walk through the pines of Millbuie. There is an information centre at Backstand, off the B9160, three miles north-west of Fortrose. A great place for a family holiday as it is on the "dry" side of the country. Sea, forest, accessibility to other areas, plenty of little towns, golf courses and all these walks to choose from. A book, *Walks on the Black Isle* is available from Muir of Ord Tourist Information Centre, Muir of Ord, Ross-shire, *Tel* Muir of Ord 433.

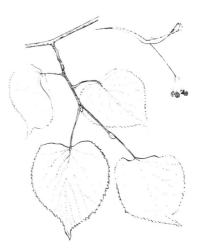

*Opposite: the Scottish Wildcat. Numbers are increasing because of food and shelter provided by new forests.*

# THE NORTH EAST

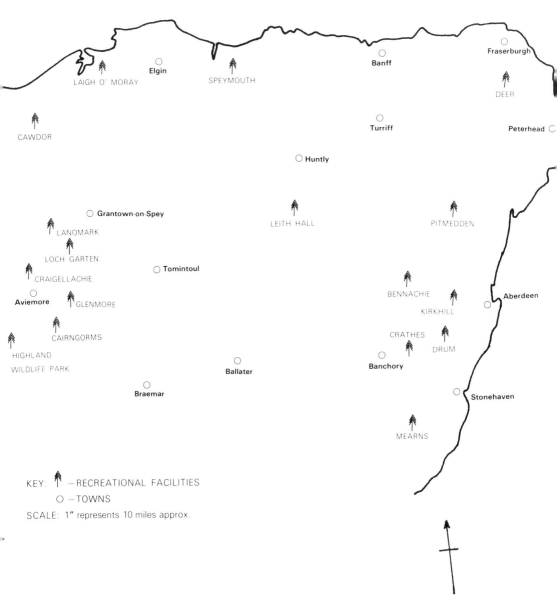

Elgin

LAIGH O' MORAY

SPEYMOUTH

Banff

Fraserburgh

DEER

CAWDOR

Turriff

Peterhead

Huntly

Grantown-on-Spey

LANDMARK

LOCH GARTEN

CRAIGELLACHIE

Aviemore

GLENMORE

Tomintoul

LEITH HALL

PITMEDDEN

BENNACHIE

KIRKHILL

Aberdeen

CRATHES

DRUM

CAIRNGORMS

HIGHLAND
WILDLIFE PARK

Ballater

Banchory

Braemar

Stonehaven

MEARNS

KEY: ⬆ —RECREATIONAL FACILITIES

○ — TOWNS

SCALE: 1″ represents 10 miles approx.

# The North East

This, my last area, is probably the most complex. It is an area of thriving farms and is the homeland of modern plantation forestry. It encompasses the rich, green growing lands of Buchan and The Garioch to the Arctic Tundra that is the Cairngorm Plateau. The Cairngorms are the highest area of land in Scotland, and from it many rivers and their agriculturally rich straths radiate down to a broad coastal plain.

Forestry has always been important in this area and the old, original forests were not cleared until after the more lowland woods had gone. The landowners eagerly applied themselves to creating new forests in the seventeenth and eighteenth centuries. It was largely due to their efforts that this country could find timber during the two wars of this century. Much planting has been done since the Forestry Commission was founded but, to this day, fifty-four per cent of all woodlands are privately owned.

The western boundary of this area lies to the west of the A9 so it is appropriate that we begin in the valley of the Upper Spey, using Aviemore as our centre.

## Aviemore

Aviemore now provides the complete holiday package, from luxury hotels to simple campsite and bothy amid unique scenery. It has a huge range of facilities: skiing, skating, curling, cinemas, sailing, swimming, climbing, exhibitions, discos, bars and anything else you would expect to find in a large centre. Its main appeal, however, lies in its natural suroundings and the opportunity for everyone to enjoy themselves in quiet country pursuits or by slaloming down the White Lady ski run at sixty miles an hour.

# Glenmore Forest Park

This park was designated as such in 1948 and is, at 2600 hectares, the smallest of the National Forest Parks. It lies to the east of Aviemore with Loch Morlich at its centre and the summit of Cairn Gorm at its southern boundary. The facilities offered are:

**Glenmore Campsite**  This Class A campsite is situated on the east end of Loch Morlich. Take the A915 at Aviemore, then bear right at Coylumbridge. There are plenty of signs so you should not get lost. The site is open all year and has 220 pitches. Unfortunately, there are no facilities for the disabled and no advance booking arrangements, but with such a large campsite these are not really required. The site is acquiring a mature look now and although it may be very busy at peak times there is much to do within the site environs and the surrounding woods.

**Information Centre**  Just above the campsite is a useful information centre with a good supply of literature and plenty of local information about the park.

**Fishing**  Brown trout fishing available in Loch Morlich. Permits and boats from campsite warden.

**Sailing**  Sailing is available on the loch at *Loch Morlich Water Sports Centre, Tel* 047986 221.

**Forest Trails**  There are three trails which all start from the campsite. A leaflet, which is essential for its information, is available from either the site warden or information centre. The trails are:

**Shore Trail**  An easy one and a quarter mile walk which starts at Beach Car Park but goes through the campsite. Plenty of alternative paths.

Another easy one and a quarter mile walk which is a continuation of the Shore Trail. Main features are remnants of the Old Caledonian Pine Forest.

**Pinewood Trail**

This starts at the information centre and is an easy three-mile walk through an interesting variety of forest. Good views southwards to Coire Cas, Coire Na Ciste and Cairngorm.

**The River Trail**

Obtain a pack from the information centre. The start is threequarters of a mile up the chairlift road. Well worth attempting. (For a fuller description see Glentress Forest Wayfaring Course.)

**Wayfaring Course**

Five longer waymarked walks for the better equipped, fitter walker. Range from three to five miles. All start at Information centre and go to such places as Ryovan Pass with its fairy lochan (An Lochan Uaine) and Meall a'Buachaille (Shepherd's Hill).

**Glenmore Forest Treks**

Excellent hill walking and climbing for the experienced exist within the park area and in the neighbouring Cairngorm National Nature Reserve. The climatic conditions on the high tops can change dramatically and are no place for the inexperienced. If you would like to go up a mountain but lack the experience or the stamina, use the Cairngorm Chairlift which operates on good days during the summer (*Tel* 047986 261). You can even have a meal in Scotland's highest eating place, the Ptarmigan Restaurant.

**Climbing**

In such a busy area you will have to be experienced to be able to watch the wildlife which lives in the forest, but you should see squirrels, cross-bills and possibly crested tits. Other animals will be a bit more difficult to find. There is a reindeer herd which the owners allow you to visit with the herder. Enquiries: The Keeper, Reindeer Company Ltd., Aviemore, Inverness-shire, *Tel* 047 486 228. The herd has been there since 1954; I remember one memorable night when the reindeer marched in single file to the top of conical Airgiod-Meall.

**Wildlife**

The whole shore of Loch Morlich has virtually been turned into one continuous car park and picnic site. It

**Picnic Sites**

127

has been well effected by the retention of plenty of birch, alder and Scots Pine so you can, with a little effort, find privacy. Loch Morlich has a lovely sandy beach for children to play but remember that the loch is at 1100 feet (335 metres) above sea level and that its water comes from melting snow for most of the year, so it will be cold and care should be exercised. Toilet facilities are also provided.

**Norwegian Hostel**  Built in commemoration of the Norwegian Forces who trained here during the war, this attractive wooden building replaced the two original huts. It sleeps 48 and can be hired by youth groups and other organisations. Contact: Forestry Commission, 6 Queen's Gate, Aberdeen AB9 2NQ.

# Cairngorm National Nature Reserve

Neighbouring the Forest Park to the east is the *Cairngorm National Nature Reserve*. It is the country's biggest reserve at 26,000 hectares and the work being done there is explained at a Visitor Centre at Loch An Eilean where there is a car park and nature trail round a beautiful loch with a ruined castle on its island (eilean) which was a stronghold of the notorious Wolf of Badenoch. It can be found one and a quarter miles off the B970 Inverdruie to Insh road just about a mile from its junction with the A951. In conjunction with a visit to the above I suggest you visit the Highland Guides Information Bureau at Inverdruie which is run by the Local District Council where there is a car park, picnic place, and displays; here you can meet and talk with Rothiemurchus Ranger Service. They also have a picnic place at *Moormore* with paths to the River Luineag. A well produced leaflet and a map are available from both places.

# Craigellachie National Nature Reserve

Located on the hillside to the east of Aviemore. Access is gained on foot from the Aviemore Centre. Managed by the Nature Conservancy Council. Contact, *Tel* 0479 810477 for both reserves.

To the south of Aviemore the Forestry Commission has *Feshiebridge Picnic Place*. Situated in open pinewoods there is a children's play area and a short walk for a view of the Cairngorms. Off the B970 Inverdruie to Insh road at Feshiebridge.

**Rock Woods Picnic Place and Trail**

Situated beside a picturesque group of small lochans there is a one-mile trail with interpretative boards. Great views.

**Tolvah Picnic Place**

Both Tolvah and Rock Woods can be found on the unclassified road to Glen Feshie off the B970.

# Highland Wildlife Park

Located at Kincraig on the old A9, this is worth a visit just to see the animals which live, or once lived, in the Highlands.

# Landmark Centre

To the north there are two main recreational facilities. The first is the *Landmark Centre* at Carrbridge on the old A9. This is a commercial tourist attraction which has a large shop, restaurant, toilets, snack bar, theatre, film displays and two very short trails concerned with nature and sculpture and numerous abstract works are located through the scattered large Scots Pine. An excellent introduction to the area.

*Loch Garten Nature Reserve* is managed by the Royal Society for the Protection of Birds. This reserve is famous as the first nesting eyrie that the Osprey used when it returned to this country. There is a shop, an observation hide, pleasant walks and information displays. Located at Loch Garten threequarters of a mile north of the Boat of Garten road junction. Contact, *Tel* 047 983 648

Our route now is to follow the Spey northwards through fine, well-managed forests mostly belonging to the Seafield Estates, to Grantown-on-Spey where we turn north to the Laigh O'Moray. There to the east lies *Cawdor Castle* which is open to the public and has a shop, restaurant, nature trails, fine policies and other attractions. In the centre of the region lies the *Laigh O'Moray Forest*, a large, mainly pinewood, forest. There are two, well-constructed and laid out picnic sites.

**Torrieston Picnic Place**  Located on the unclassified road to Pluscarden Abbey off the B9010 from Elgin there are a series of walks from under a mile to two miles through tall, mature timber. There are toilets beside the picnic place. The site is maintained in conjunction with Moray District Council.

**Roseisle Picnic Place**  Off the B7089 Kinloss to Burghead road this busy picnic site abuts onto miles of sandy beaches, but the site is sheltered by its trees. The pines growing on the sand hereabouts are Corsican Pine and have proved adaptable to growing in sand and assisting in stabilising sand dune movement. Toilets with disabled facilities available.

# Speymouth Forest

We move eastwards on the A96 to *Speymouth Forest* passing through good arable land with plenty of plantations indicative of the area's forestry history. Once again there are two picnic sites and walks of a high standard.

**Winding Walks Picnic Place**  Located off the A98 Fochabers to Buckie road, one mile east of Fochabers. This large car park and picnic site with toilets is situated amid splendid woodland scenery.

A series of walks lead off which will cater for everyone's needs, from a few hundred yards in length to two and a half miles with views of the River Spey and the Moray Coast from Peeps Gazebo.

**Ault Dearg Picnic Place**

Located one and a half miles due south of Fochabers on an unclassified road, this small car park has fine views of the River Spey with its one and a half mile walk along the riverside. There are views of the unique "Earth Pillars" above the Spey.

For those of you who drive over the "Lecht" to Upper Don and Deeside, there is a series of country walks in Tomintoul, Scotland's second highest village at 1120 feet (341 metres). (The highest village is actually Wanlockhead in the Lowther Hills, South Scotland.) Glen Livet Forest has been planted primarily to provide timber but with the provision of shelter for both farming and shooting a high priority. Hence the smaller blocks of plantations.

# Forest of Deer

Back on the coastal plain our next forest is the *Forest of Deer* in the heart of the Buchan.

**White Cow Wood Picnic Place and Walks**

Located on a minor road linking Sticken on the A981 with the A950 just west of Deer Abbey. The picnic place is situated under beech trees. There is a children's play area and toilets with facilities for the disabled. Two walks lead from there: *Red Walk* An easy walk of one mile through plantations of spruce and larch. *Yellow Walk* Another easy, but longer, walk at three miles length.

**Pony Trekking**

This can be arranged with a local stables through Loudon Wood. Contact, Forestry Commission, Lynwood, Pitfour, Mintlaw, Peterhead, *Tel* 07714 265.

Turn off the main road to the Forest of Deer, the main (A96) road which goes through Huntly Forest, an older forest of pinewoods with a large harvesting programme. In this area are many fine outstanding trees. Many of them are in the care of the National Trust.

## Pitmedden Gardens

On the A920 between Ellon and Old Meldrum. Primarily a formal Jacobean walled garden, but with a woodland walk attached which is quite pleasant.

## Leith Hall

On the B9002 seven miles south of Huntly. This house has especially fine policies. Guided walks available.

## Crathes and Drum Castles

Both these castles are in Deeside. Drum is about ten miles from Aberdeen, off the A93 while Crathes is a further five miles on up the glen just east of Banchory. With these two castles and Leith Hall the Trust has 400 hectares of policies with many fine walks. In Drum there is a one and a half mile walk through the Old Forest of Drum which is a Birch, Oak, and Scots Pine wood with an underplanting of exotic shrubs.

At Crathes there are four walks all with a forestry content. Guide book, restaurant, gardens and a ranger service available. Contact, *Tel* 033 044 651.

In the vicinity of Aberdeen there are four forests with extensive recreational facilities. These are Bennachie, Kirkhill, Banchory and Mearns. All are used primarily by locals and provide a convenient lung for a busy city. The area is, however, a popular holiday area. The two southern forests probably offer the tourist more scenic value.

# Bennachie Forest

This is the nearest big hill to Aberdeen and is much patronised by the city's residents. There are three car parks encircling the hills, from which a series of walks and longer linking walks start. All the car parks are on minor roads between the A96 and A944 and are quite difficult to find.

**Don View Visitor Centre**

On the minor road from Kenmay to Keig. I suggest the long way round might be the simplest. Use the A944 to Whitehouse, turn right onto B992 Insch road. After three or four miles turn right at Keig after crossing the River Don. Another four miles or so should bring you to the car park where there is an information centre, toilets (with facilities for the disabled), a picnic place overlooking the Don, and two walks. *Red Walk*, an easy half-mile walk on forest road and in woodland. *Blue Walk*, a longer, more strenuous, three mile circular walk through the forest and onto the top of Millstone Hill with fine views of Mither Tap (1733 feet, 528 metres). From the top a further five miles will take you to Back o' Bennachie car park, while another route of four and a half miles will take you to Esson's car park; but these walks are only for the fit.

**Esson's Car Park**

On an unclassified road about a mile and a half south of Chapel of Garioch. Car park with picnic place and toilets with facilities for the disabled. Two walks: *White Walk*, an easy one-mile through plantations. *Yellow Walk*, actually two walks described under blue walk from Don View.

**Back o' Bennachie Car Park**

Off the B9002 road to Insch. The car park is signposted. It is large, with a picnic area with children's play area, toilets and three varied walks. *White*, short on a good surface. *Purple*, an easy walk through plantations. *Yellow*, the climb to the top of Mither Tap and beyond to the other car parks.

# Kirkhill Forest

Located just to the east of Aberdeen, practically in the suburbs. There is a series of car parks in pleasant mixed woodlands with fine walks through broadleaves and conifers. Bridle paths have also been laid down for which a permit is required by those wishing to ride in the forest. Contact the Forestry Commission, *Tel 022 476 259*. There is also a short wayfaring course at Tyrebagger plantation. Contact, the Forestry Commission, 6 Queen's Gate, Aberdeen (during office hours) or from *Blackburn Filling Station*.

All these facilities are difficult to find as they lie on a series of minor roads (with inadequate signposting) between the A93 and A944.

# Banchory Forest

Farther up Deeside is this fine forest with attractive scenery.

**Shooting Greens** Shooting Greens can be found on a minor road linking the B993 and B974. The latter is the Banchory to Fettercairn road; the former links the A93 with the B976 which runs along the south bank of the Dee. There are toilets (with facilities for the disabled), a picnic area in an elevated position with views of the Dee, and a range of three walks through mixed woodland with fine views of Deeside and the high hills of the Grampians behind. Can be steep and rough in places.

**Mulloch** On an unclassified road to the west of the A957 Banchory to Stonehaven road (called Slug Road). A small picnic place with views over the Feugh valley and the Kincardine Hills. There is a short walk through larch plantations.

# Mearns Forest

There is a picnic place with a short walk through mixed woodland past a pond and a stream. This is a good spot for watching wildlife, so remember to be quiet. Located on the minor road from Auchenblae to Clatterin Brig in Drumtochty Glen. Toilets available with facilities for the disabled. Pony trekking can be arranged. Contact, the Forestry Commission, *Tel* 056 12 284.

To complete my coverage of this north east area I would be remiss if I did not direct you up *Deeside* with its Royal Castle and undoubted scenic attractions. It is also richly wooded and provided you exercise great care there is scope for short informal walks close to the road. There are three major remnants of the old Caledonian Forest at Glentanner, Ballochbuie and Mar. These can only be viewed from the road as their owners are carefully managing these woods so as to increase their size by using existing parent stock. At Dinnet there is a National Nature Reserve. Contact, *Tel* 033 985 369. Close by Ballater the climb up through the oaks of Craigendarroch (rock hill of the oaks) will provide a splendid panorama of forest and mountain. For the hill walker and mountaineer this is a magnetic area with approaches to Lochnagar, Cairngorms, Beinn a' Bhuird and countless long-distance mountain walks.

For further information visit any of the local information centres in any of the towns or purchase any of the detailed guides of the locality. I would naturally recommend the Forestry Commission guide — *Forests of North East Scotland*, which is packed with useful information.

You should leave this wonderful area by travelling on the A93 over the Cairnwell, a skiing centre, and the now tamed Devil's Elbow to Perth and so to the south. When the need fo refresh your body and soul next arises the quietness and the peacefulness off the beaten track in Scotland's forests will be there to do just that.

*A Hen Harrier with her young at the nest: taken in Fearnoch Forest.*

# III

# The
# Trees

# Conifers

This large group of trees, also known as softwood trees, is very important because it can produce a large volume of wood on poor wet soils. Because of the traditional imports of softwood from the Baltic states and Canada the trade is orientated towards conifers. The wood is easily worked and has a long length of fibre, therefore it is in demand for building, fencing, pallets, boxes, transmission poles, and mining timber. The long fibre length makes it the principal timber for processing into paper and chipboard.

A conifer has a distinct set of characteristics. These are:

1   A narrow needle-like or scale-like leaf.
2   Evergreen foliage (there are exceptions to this).
3   Buds with a covering of paper-like scales.
4   Conical shape with regular branching habit (known as whorls of branches).
5   "Piney" fragrance due to production of resin.
6   Trees are dual sexed and carry both male and female flowers.
7   Pollen is borne by the wind so male flowers are always catkin-like.
8   The seeds are always small, produced in a cone, and are usually winged.
9   Seedlings have numerous seed leaves or cotyledons.

Conifers form the bulk of species found in Scottish plantations because they grow so well in our wet climate and the trade will always be conifer-orientated. The importation of West Coast American species last century, and their subsequent large-scale use this century has been forced on us by a ninety-two per cent reliance on imported wood in a growing market, a shrinking natural forest, and the inability to organise a recyclable commodity in a market economy.

# Spruces

There are three spruces used in Scottish forestry. These are Sitka Spruce, Norway Spruce and Omorika Spruce. Sitka Spruce is the most important conifer in commercial forestry in this country, while Norway Spruce was extensively planted in older plantations and is currently ranking fourth. Omorika Spruce is very rarely planted and I have included it only because if you find a spruce which you cannot identify as Sitka or Norway it will most probably be Omorika.

The common characteristics of spruces are that they all grow in the Northern Hemisphere and their leaves or needles grow on short pegs which give their shoots a roughness to touch. They all have a plate-like shallow root structure which under certain circumstances makes them liable to be blown over by the wind (called windblow).

The West of Scotland is an excellent area to grow spruces with some remarkable growth rates being achieved. There are about 300,000 hectares of spruce plantations in Scotland yielding on average, say, 200 cubic metres at a standing value of around £8 per metre. The resulting value of the timber would be £480 million. A calculation like the one above is always difficult but it gives you some idea of the value of our forests.

# Sitka Spruce

This tree is the one most planted by foresters in Scotland because it is the fastest growing and yields the most timber over the widest range of sites. It was introduced to this country by the Scottish botanist David Douglas in 1831. The tree's natural distribution is from Kodiak Island in Alaska down a narrow coastal strip through British Columbia, Washington, and Oregon to Northern California. In Scotland where its distribution is almost universal most of the planting stock has been raised with seed from British Columbia. The exceptions

*Sitka Spruce*

to this universal distribution are the very dry east, and the acid peat bogs of the north.

The tree almost always grows in the classic conifer shape of a pyramid. The needles which grow on little hard pegs are dark, shiny green above with a bluish-white underside giving the tree a blue look, especially when viewed in a plantation.

The bark is dark brown, and in older trees breaks up into flat plates which have curly edges. Another characteristic of mainly older trees is the growth of epicormic shoots direct from the trunk. Its branching habit is of regularly spaced whorls or clusters of branches which usually indicate the main growth of that year, although if you are trying to age spruce by counting the whorls you should be careful not to count in the lammas growth. Lammas growth is the additional growth into autumn which usually takes the shape of an extra whorl of small branches, and in a good year produces another twenty-five centimetres of growth. Cones are produced infrequently but are seven centimetres long, pale brown with wavy scales. The timber is the premier wood for processing into something else like paper or cardboard. This is because it is white, has a long fibre, and is easily worked by the debarking and chipping machines. It is also sawn into building timber and wood for pallets.

If you are walking through a plantation of large sitka spruce about forty years old, it will have a standing volume of anything from 350 to 600 cubic metres depending on how it has been managed. This is about twenty articulated lorry loads of sawlogs worth around £8000 and ten loads to the paper-maker worth around £2500. It will take six workers using chainsaws about a month and a half to cut it down and another man with a large extraction machine about a week and a half to bring it to the forest roadside.

# Norway Spruce

*Norway Spruce*

This tree, the traditional Christmas tree, was introduced to this country around 1500. It has extensive natural range covering all of mainland Europe north of the

Alps, the Carpathian Mountains, and the Balkans, stretching right into Russia. There is speculation that it would have been native in this country if the Channel "Land Bridge" had been in existence longer.

In this country Norway Spruce can be found in all localities. Most older forests have extensive plantations of this species, as it was considered the safe species to plant right up to World War II, when Sitka spruce proved itself superior. Everyone who buys a real Christmas tree should be able to recognise a young Norway Spruce by its fresh, shiny, dark green needles which feel soft in comparison to Sitka. In older trees the most striking characteristic is the reddish-brown smooth bark. It produces cylindrical curved cones about fifteen to twenty centimetres long.

Norway is now only planted in either favoured situations such as good ground for Christmas trees, where Sitka will not grow, that is, in frost hollows where Sitka will be damaged by spring frosts.

The timber of the Norway Spruce is put to the same use as that of Sitka, but because it usually grows more slowly, quality logs can be converted to finishing timber. This spruce does not yield the same quantity of wood per hectare as Sitka, therefore a hectare of forty-year-old Norway will only produce 200 to 450 cubic metres of timber, or around fifteen large lorry loads.

# Scots Pine

This is our only native conifer of any importance. Remnants of the old indigenous stands of this species can be found throughout the Highlands of Scotland, and for those of you who wish to pursue the subject I suggest you read *The Native Pinewoods of Scotland* by H. M. Steven and A.C. Carlisle. However, the principal areas open to the general public are from north to south: *Loch Maree*—Beinn Eighe Nature Reserve: *Glen Affric*—Forestry Commission: *Glen More*—Rothiemurchus Nature Reserve: *Blackwood of Rannoch*—Forestry Commission.

The official policy of the Forestry Commission is *1*. To conserve the undisturbed development of the pinewood

*Scots Pine*

ecosystem in all the areas of existing pinewood. *2.* To secure natural regeneration of the existing pinewood. *3.* To extend the existing native pinewood on to contiguous areas. *4.* To prevent contamination of the local genetic types.

The Commission follow this policy in areas in their ownership, and encourage private owners by providing a planting grant. In my list of woods to visit, two are under the direct management of the Nature Conservancy. These are managed to protect examples of the range of British wildlife and wild places. Native birch and oak woods, pine forests, lochs and river systems, peat bogs and mountain tops are included in their schemes. These are places where positive steps can be taken to maintain or even create the right conditions for our natural wildlife. The Nature Conservancy Council can help owners of native woodlands with grants to help conserve them.

But what of the tree itself? The range of Scots pine is immense, from Spain, France, and Scotland across Northern Europe and Siberia to the Pacific Ocean, with an outlier in the Caucasus Mountains. In Scotland it has been used extensively in plantations in north and east Scotland where the conditions of light soils and a dryish climate are ideal. It has been planted in the west on a very limited scale.

The characteristics common to all types of Scots pine are the orange-red bark in the upper crown in trees over ten years old, and the glaucous blue-grey needles which are borne in pairs. The form of young trees is conic but in older trees an "umbrella" form is very common. With age the bark becomes deeply fluted and cracked. It also becomes much darker and thicker, a fact that has probably saved some of our native remnants from fire damage. The cones take two years to ripen and are roughly conical in shape; about five centimetres long, they have diamond-shaped scales which have two raised spines crossing them. Pines do not have any internodal branching so you can easily estimate a tree's age by counting the whorls of branches.

The timber of this tree is the "redwood" of the timber trade and has been imported in large quantities from Scandinavia and Russia over many years. It is the principal wood used in the building trade, and for railway sleepers, transmission poles and fencing. Because it is a relatively slow grower and poor producer (six to fourteen cubic metres per annum) it is increasingly being replaced by the volume-producing Sitka spruce. It still represents, however, about ten to twelve per cent of our Scottish woodlands.

## General location of natural Scots Pine stands

| | |
|---|---|
| *Deeside* | Glentanar, Ballochbuie and Mar |
| *Speyside* | Abernethy, Rothiemurchus, Glenmore, Glen Feshie, Dulnain, and Glen Avon |
| *Rannoch* | Black Wood of Rannoch, the Old Wood of Meggernie |
| *Great Glen* | Glens Moriston, Loyne, Garry, Mallie, Loy, Nevis, Barrisdale, Loch Arkaig, and Ardgour |
| *Strath Glas* | Glens Affric, Cannich, Strathfarrar, and Guisachan |
| *Wester Ross* | Loch Maree, Coulin, Achnashellach, and Shieldaig |
| *Northern* | Amat, Rhidorroch, Glen Einig, and Strath Vaich |
| *Southern* | Black Mount, Glens Orchy, Falloch, and Strath Fillan |

This list may seem large but most of these can only be called remnants. There are, for example, only about twenty-four trees in Glen Falloch.

You should also remember that in all of these woods some rehabilitation may be taking place, so check with the person in charge before you enter unless, of course, you are following a forest trail.

# Lodge Pole Pine

*Lodgepole Pine*

This pine has been extensively planted on the very poorest peat bogs throughout Scotland from Galloway to Caithness. Early experiments had shown that this tree will grow over a huge variety of sites and it was decided to use it as a pioneer species on the poor ground which was being made available for forestry from the mid-fifties to the present day. Its use is still the subject of debate among foresters, as some doubt exists as to whether it will produce worthwhile timber for harvesting. A further doubt has been sown by a widespread attack of epidemic proportions by a moth known as pine beauty moth.

Lodgepole pine's natural range is from Alaska to California but within this range are two distinct varieties which are difficult to tell apart. If you are standing in the middle of green two-needled pines on a Scottish peat bog you are among lodgepole pine. The main characteristics of this tree are the shoots which are around three centimetres long. During March they lengthen to six to fifteen centimetres, when they show off the contortions from which the tree is named. The needles are longer than the Scots pine, are green with a dark red-brown basal sheath and usually have a twist in them. The bark is a dullish red-brown colour throughout its life, smooth when younger but becoming fissured when older. The shape varies from being bushy to a thin narrow pyramid depending on the tree's origin. The cones and flowers are conspicuously and abundantly borne from an early age. The cones differ from Scots pine by having a little prickle in the centre of the scale.

The timber to date has not been extensively harvested, but it is expected to be similar to that of Scots pine. Incidentally, the American Indians are reputed to have used it as a pole for their wigwams, hence the name "Lodgepole." Like most pines it is a poor producer (four to fourteen cubic metres per annum) but its usefulness as a pioneer species makes it about six per cent of Scotland's tree cover.

# Corsican Pine

This pine is only very occasionally planted in Scotland. I have included it because it is extensively used in coastal plantings on the Moray Firth at Culbin and a few other places. It comes from Corsica and, as can be seen from the specific name, is a variety of *Pinus nigra*, the Austrian pine. It was introduced in 1759 and has over the years replaced the Scots Pine in south-eastern English plantations, such as Thetford Chase.

*Corsican Pine*

A tree with a conic shape and light branches, it has two pale green needles which are twisted and spread widely apart. They are softer and more slender than the other two pines I have described. The bark is fissured of a grey and pink coloration which develops into darker coloured plates when old. The cone is larger than the other two at six to seven centimetres. The wood is less dense than Scots and therefore is not used as much in the building trade, but is preferred by the chipboard, woodwool and pulp processors. The bark is now being processed for the horticultural trade as a soil conditioner. It can outyield Scots pine (six to twenty cubic metres per annum), but because of its climatic limitations will not be extensively planted in Scotland.

# European Larch, Hybrid Larch, Japanese Larch

I have included the three larches in one section as they are all broadly similar. They are all deciduous conifers which lose their needles in November. To explain their position I will have to give you an insight into their history. European larch was introduced into this country by the Scottish botanist Menzies in 1737. Some of these trees were planted at Dunkeld for the Duke of Atholl and were destined to become the progenitors of all the pre-1900 plantings of this species in Scotland.

*European Larch*

145

*Japanese Larch*

Some of the offspring of these trees were also to become the parents of Hybrid larch which was discovered in 1904. Because of the enthusiasm of Victorian planters larch is extensively used in estate forestry in the traditional forestry areas where the ground and weather conditions are suitable. With the expansion of forestry into the poorer wetlands of the west, Japanese larch was used to a greater extent. Larch planting had passed its peak by the early 1960s as modernisation of coal mining was completed. Larch, with its speedy growth in its early years, was thought to be the ideal pit prop. It is now mostly used for landscaping purposes when its winter habit can be used to good effect to underline a prominent natural feature such as a spur of a hill.

The trees lose their needles in the winter, when the inexpert can tell European by the colour of the shoots. European has pale creamy-grey ones while Japanese has shoots of a russet colour. Hybrid is intermediate and is usually described as straw-coloured. All grow light green needles in rosettes on the older shoots while the needles are grown singly on the current year's shoot. The bark shows to some extent the same colour gradation and becomes on all species deeply fissured when old. Except on old estate trees all species will have a conic appearance. The cones vary a lot, even within the same species, but are usually about three centimetres long. Those of European have adpressed cone scales while Japanese have reflexed scales, and the natural hybrid is intermediate. The timber of European is very durable outdoors without preservative and it therefore is much used in boatbuilding and all kinds of fencing and general outdoor applications. If you see large, widely-spaced trees with bowed butts these are being specially grown as boatskin larch and will fetch high prices. Larches represent about eight per cent of Scottish plantations because of the reasons I have explained, despite their low yields of six to fourteen cubic metres per annum.

# Douglas Fir

This tree was introduced to this country by the Scottish botanist, David Douglas, in 1827. The scientific name

146

commemorates another Scottish botanist, Archibald Menzies, who discovered the tree in 1791. It was a very popular introduction and was extensively planted in policy woods throughout the country where they are now Scotland's tallest trees with heights of over fifty metres.

The natural distribution is from Northern British Columbia to California. Most Scottish seed comes from stands in British Columbia and Vancouver Island, where the tree grows to a height of seventy-five metres. In this country it grows best on sheltered mid-valley slopes with a deep soil such as can be found at Glentress. As a plantation tree it requires careful management so that any good stands you find are as a result of dedicated thinning over the years.

*Douglas Fir*

The tree can be recognised by its deeply fissured bark when older, the soft green needles, which pulled from the stem leave a smooth round scar and release a strong fruity smell, and the slender "beech-like" buds. When grown on the correct site it is a big producer of quality wood, which can be used for construction work and plywood manufacture. The timber is known as "Oregon" or "Columbian" pine.

# The Silver Firs

## Grand Fir, Noble Fir

These two trees, though not seen extensively as plantation trees, are very frequently planted in small patches in most forests and policies, for both are very high volume producers and good lookers.

Grand fir can be recognised by the smooth bark and flat spread of green needles on the shoot. Noble fir is recognised by its up-curving bluish needles. It, too, has a smooth bark and can be seen in August and September sporting large green upright cones near the top of the tree. Both trees have resin blisters on the bark, and you should take care if you burst one that you do not get a

*Grand Fir*

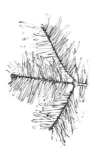

squirt of resin in the eye. The timber from both these trees is of poor quality and generally not required by the timber trade. The foliage of Noble fir is much sought after for Christmas decorations in Denmark and Germany. If (and it is very unlikely) you are offered one of these trees as a Christmas tree, do snap it up as it will fill your room with a beautiful resinous smell and not shed one single needle.

# Wellingtonia, Coast Redwood

*Wellingtonia*

Both these trees are renowned for their great size in the natural groves in Northern California. Wellingtonia has produced the biggest tree in the world in Northern California, which is about 84 metres tall, 31 metres round at the base, and is estimated to weigh 2145 tonnes. The species produces big trees in this country, too, and I would recommend you if you can to visit the Younger Gardens at Benmore near Dunoon where you will see a magnificent avenue of such trees.

# Lawson's Cypress, Western Red Cedar

*Lawson's Cypress*

These two need no introduction to the gardeners among you; both have feathery foliage which is aromatic when bruised. To tell them apart you should run your fingers over the tips of the leafy twigs. The cedar will feel stout and firm while the cypress will be slender and droopy. Both species will be found either under broadleaves or in roadside plantings. The timber of neither plays any part in the trade, but they are durable outdoors so much so that the cabins at Strathyre are made of the wood of the Japanese cedar *Cryptomeria japonica*. The wood of

Thuja is much sought after by woodcutters in British Columbia and there is perhaps a future for this species in this country's forests.

## Juniper, Yew

These are our two remaining indigenous conifers. The yew to the forest visitor is the least important as it is rarely seen outside our larger policies. Mention should be made of the Yew at Fortingall which is reputed to have been there when Pontius Pilate was born there.

*Yew*

The juniper is probably more important as it is widespread throughout the Highlands. It is common in the pine forests of the north east where its prickly three-spined needles can give you a sore jab. If you find one, crush a few needles or berries and smell the aroma of gin. Juniper berries are used to flavour this liquor.

# Broadleaves

Broadleaves are trees which are part of the plant order called dicotyledons, that is, plants which have two seeds leaves or cotyledons in every seed. However, for the non-botanically minded I prefer the easier definition which is: a tree which has broad leaves, sheds them in the winter, and has a generally rounded haphazard way of growing. This is unlike most conifers which have a conic shape and regular branching patterns. Broadleaves in this country can be split into two main groups — indigenous and introduced.

### Indigenous

This group consists of *oak, ash, birch, hazel, rowan, aspen, willow, wild cherry, holly* and *elm*. These in one or other grouping of species covered most of the Lowlands of Scotland. On higher or harsher sites they were replaced by *Scots Pine* with or without *birch*. It is a fascinating vision of how, as the ice retreated and the weather grew warmer, coloniser species such as birch and Scots Pine slowly spread northwards. To be in turn followed and replaced by the growing mass of oak, ash, and hazel woods up the valleys from the coastal plains. This is the forest of much of Europe and Asia which has, especially in Scotland, been overcut, burned and removed by man.

You can trace this ancient forest in the fragments that have been left. These are always in the wilder and more inaccessible parts of the west and north, or steep glens and gorges such as some of the Clyde Valley gorges. At the Wood of Cree, and Glen Trool in Galloway, there are important remnants. Most of the wilder looking broadleaved woodlands in Argyll are fragments and mention should be made of the Nature Conservancy reserve at Glen Nant near Taynuilt where there is a descriptive trail. Moving across country you find birchwoods and pinewoods beginning to dominate. Examples of the former can be found on Tummelside and Killiecrankie while Rothiemurchus is an outstanding example of the latter.

*Sessile Oak*

# Oak, Sessile, Pedunculate

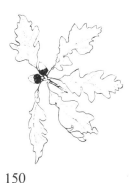

These two trees are given together, and although botanists have adequately defined the two species it is difficult to tell them apart, because at no one time can all the decisive differences be seen.

In most of Scotland the indigenous woods are populated with sessile oak, while park and policy trees will possibly be pedunculate. All oaks have curiouly lobed leaves and clusters of buds, they produce acorns which, in medieval times, were important as a source of food for pigs. The stripping of acorns was known as pannage, and a rent was duly charged. It also inhibited the regeneration of the wood. Oaks are one of the last trees to produce their leaves in the spring and there is a rhyme which says

> Oak before Ash
> Then we'll surely have a splash.
> Ash before Oak
> Then we must have a soak.

Either way it seems to me we suffer!

The wild oakwoods you see on the sides of Lochs Awe, Fyne, and Lomond have all been intensively managed on a coppice system to provide charcoal for iron smelters set up in Vale of Leven, Bonawe, and Furnace. While that type of management has resulted in a degraded wood today, the main depredation has come from the spring burning techniques carried out by the sheep farmer to provide a fresh early bite.

*Pedunculate Oak*

# Ash

Ash grows everywhere that there is a soil deep enough to support its voracious appetite. It can be recognised by its pinnate compound leaf in the summer and its greyish twigs with black buds in the winter. Quality ash timber, of which there is very little in Scotland, is used for handles, shafts, and in making sports equipment such as hockey sticks.

*Ash*

# Hazel

Hazel can be recognised by its rounded leaf in summer, its nuts in the autumn, its catkins in early spring, and its hairy twigs in winter. It is used by shepherds to make their crooks, and crookmakers are always on the lookout for straight sticks.

151

# Alder

*Alder*

There can hardly be a stream or lochside in Scotland below a thousand feet in elevation which does not have its crop of alder. This tree will always grow where it is wet, sometimes even growing out of the water during the winter. Alder, like hazel, has a rounded leaf, but it usually grows out of a short stalk which in winter is the main means of identification. This species also sports catkins (but they are much smaller than hazel), and it produces a distinctive cone-like fruit. Alder wood is used to make clog soles.

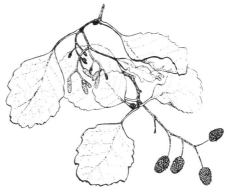

# Silver Birch, Hairy Birch

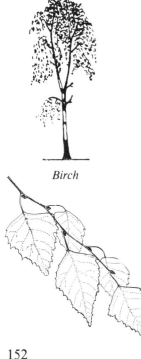

*Birch*

These two species are, again, difficult to tell apart. However, if the branches are pendulous and you are in a lowland situation with better soil, the tree will most probably be silver birch. If the branches are more upright and you are standing on a Highland hill then you are probably looking at hairy birch.

Birch can always be recognised winter and summer by its papery, whitish bark. In this country there is little use for its wood except as firewood for which it is superb. A feature of birchwood is the incidence of a bracket fungus called *Polyporous betulinus* which frequently attacks weaker trees.

# Rowan

The rowan tree can be found everywhere throughout Scotland because it has been widely planted beside houses to help protect the occupants from witches. The scattering of the seed and hardy nature of the tree have spread it near and far. It can be recognised by its six or seven pairs of leaflets growing alternately on a small bush-like tree in summer and its large dark purple alternate buds in the winter. The berries can be used to make jelly.

*Rowan*

# Willow Goat

There are many types, species and hybrids within this large genus. All share similar characteristics and I am only going to describe the most common found wild in Scotland which is the Goat Willow so called because goats like to browse on its leaves.

Willows can be found in most wet places throughout the country. They are usually a small shrub which can be recognised by its oval leaves. Tinkers traditionally used willow to make baskets, though the commercial basket maker would use a type called osiers which are specially grown for the purpose.

*White Willow*

153

# Holly

Everyone knows the holly with its sharp, wavy dark green leaves and red berries. It is a true native and may be found growing wild in the western half of the country. There are other genetic types and introduced varieties which have been planted in a semi-wild position in the large policies. Holly trees are evergreen deciduous trees with special transpiration systems to survive the winter, such as the waxy shiny leaves. Sharp spines to discourage browsing animals have developed on these leaves.

If you want to collect berries for Christmas please make the effort to take the smallest shoots so that there are berries another year as it takes eighteen months for the berries to develop.

*English Elm*

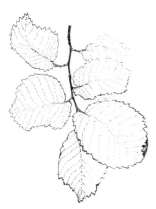

# Wych Elm

This is the native elm of Scotland which has a more or less universal distribution throughout the country, although there have been many other varieties planted in the past. Wych elm may be distinguished by its short bole, broad crown, and rough, toothed, lop-sided leaves.

Dutch elm disease did not have too devastating an effect in Scotland on the native elm. The introduced elms in such places as Edinburgh, however, were affected. Wych elm timber when it is of top quality can be used to make furniture.

## Introduced

The introduced broadleaves are commercially and probably scenically more important as most of them were planted on a large scale by the eighteenth century estate owners. These to a large extent are still in existence and being more numerous than native stands, make a greater impact on the landscape. Many forest walks are laid in broadleaves, as these are still considered to be more attractive than a coniferous forest.

# Beech

Beech was introduced from England in 1550 and planted at Newbattle, Dalkeith. It is well known with its grey, smooth bark, nuts and beautiful habit. It is an important timber tree where it can be properly grown.

*Beech*

# Sycamore

The sycamore is reputed to have been introduced direct from France by Mary, Queen of Scots who planted it at Little France in what is now a suburb of Edinburgh on the Dalkeith road. It has turned native and now can be found everywhere in Scotland where trees can grow. In Scotland it is still known by its old name of Plane, especially in the old established forestry estates of the east.

Sycamore can be recognised by its five-pointed leaves, winged seeds, and in older trees, by a reddish, orange, plated bark. Wood from this tree is, because of its white colour, still much sought after for use as veneers, making violins, and to make small wooden items such as bread boards and wooden spoons.

*Sycamore*

155

# Lime

This tree was first planted at Taymouth Castle, Kenmore, in 1664, and can be easily identified by its tall form with numerous suckers growing from the base, and large heart-shaped leaves. It has been much used as a pollarded tree for street planting. The wood is white and light and is very good for hand carving.

Laburnum, Horse Chestnut, English elm, Norway maple, Sweet Chestnut, Walnut, Poplar, Laurel, and Rhododendron were all introduced about the same time. Of these species perhaps rhododendron makes the biggest impact as it has escaped from the policies to become the dominant cover in some western areas, for example Ardentinny and Carradale. It more or less sterilises the land so no other tree can be grown.

Other introduced trees which are commonly found around our forests are Bird Cherry, contoneaster species, and Crab apple. These have been planted by foresters in an attempt to brighten things up. These trees are more suited to the urban park and are no longer being used to the same extent. Broadleaved visual relief is now provided by native species.

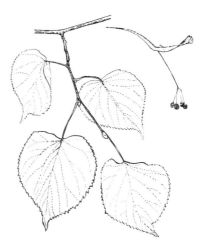

# Index